Jewish Stories and Hebrew Melodies

Engraving of Heinrich Heine in 1840 modeled after the portrait by Moritz Oppenheim, 1831

Napoleon entering Düsseldorf in 1811

Old Düsseldorf in 1794

Judengasse (Jewish Street) in the Frankfurt ghetto

The Heder (Jewish school for children), 1878 by Moritz Oppenheim (1800–1882)

A 1642 engraving of the plundering of the Frankfurt ghetto in 1614

A contemporary print of the antisemitic HEP riots in 1819; HEP stands for the antisemitic slur against Jews at the beginning of the 19th century; possibly an abbreviation for "Hierosolyma est perdita": Latin for "Jerusalem is lost."

The Rhine at the Lorelei mountain

Old Bacharach

Max Liebermann (1847–1935)

A sample page of the manuscript of The Rabbi of Bacherach by Heinrich Heine

Jewish Stories and Hebrew Melodies

by
Heinrich Heine

With a new introduction by
Elizabeth Petuchowski

ΛΛ MARKUS WIENER PUBLISHING
W New York

MASTERWORKS OF MODERN JEWISH WRITING SERIES
is issued in conjunction with the Center for the Study of the
American Jewish Experience, Hebrew Union College-Jewish
Institute of Religion, Cincinnati.

First published in the United States of America 1987 by
MARKUS WIENER PUBLISHING, INC.
2901 Broadway, New York, N.Y. 10025

Library of Congress Cataloging-in-Publication Data

Heine, Heinrich, 1797–1856.
    Jewish stories and Hebrew melodies.

    (Masterworks of modern Jewish writing series)
    Translated from the German.
    Bibliography: p.
    Contents: The Rabbi of Bacherach / translated by
Charles Godfrey Leland—Shylock / translated by
Frederic Ewen—Hebrew melodies / translated by Hal
Draper.
    1. Jews—Literary collections. 2. Judaism—Literary
collections. 3. Heine, Heinrich, 1797–1856—Transla-
tions, English. I. Title. II. Series.
PT2316.A3P47   1987   831′.7   86-40567
ISBN 0-910129-68-1
ISBN 0-910129-62-2 (pbk.)
Cover Design; Cheryl Mirkin
Printed in the United States of America

Acknowledgement

Grateful acknowlegement is made to the following for permission to reprint and adapt previously published materials

—Translation of *The Rabbi of Bacherach* from German by Charles Godfrey Leland (Hans Breitman), New York: E.P. Dutton & Co, London: Heinemann 1906. This translation was updated by Elizabeth Petuchowski in 1987.

—Translation of "Jessica" from *Shakespeare's Maidens and Women* by Heinrich Heine from German by Frederic Ewen under the new title Shylock in *The Poetry and Prose of Heinrich Heine* by Frederic Ewen. Copyright © 1948 by Citadel Press. Reprinted with permission of Citadel Press.

—Translation of *Hebrew Melodies* from German by Hal Draper (Including the footnotes). Copyright © 1982 by Hal Draper. Reprinted from *The Complete Poems of Heinrich Heine*. A Modern English Version by Hal Draper. (Originally published under the title: Poems by H. Heine. Third volume: Romanzero.) Reprinted with permission of Suhrkamp/Insel Publishers, New York and Frankfurt.

Acknowledgement for the Reproductions
of the Illustrations

The lithographs by Max Liebermann for the limited and signed edition of the Rabbi von Bacherach, published in 1923 by Propyläen Verlag, Berlin, were reproduced with permission of owner of the rights, Mrs. Marianne Feilchenfeldt, Zürich, estate of Paul Cassirer. The reproductions were made possible with the friendly assistance of the Heinrich Heine Institut, Düsseldorf. All other photos included in this volume were also provided by the Heinrich Heine Institut, Düsseldorf.

Table of Contents

Portrait of Heinrich Heine in his youth

Introduction

Heinrich Heine is "in vogue."

But which Heinrich Heine? There is Heine, the radical, super-critical and crabby, whose writings were censored together with those of other malcontents who left Germany and fulminated out of France against the land of their birth. The Marseillaise sung under his window intoxicated this Heine, its refrain sparked in his head "glowing stars of enthusiasm and rockets of mockery."

Seated opposite that Heine by the window is Heine the armchair politician and wordmonger, who was friendly with Karl Marx, saw in Jesus "the divine communist" one day, and the next complained: "A sombre, spiteful mood prevails here, and one is not safe from the most terrible outbursts. I am very much afraid of the cruelty of proletarian rule, and I must confess that out of fear I have become a conservative."

This Heine has been assessed with enviable fairness by Jeffrey L. Sammons, whose *Heinrich Heine: A Modern Biography* demonstrates how changes in political climate effect changes in Heine's political stance. For Heine did not lock himself into irrepealable extremism as he responded to the German forces of reaction or to Paris mobs. He may have viewed communism as applied messianism with one eye, but kept the other judiciously on the censor. This Heine described himself as a "Constitutionalist": "I am, strictly speaking, neither a republican, nor a monarchist. I am in favor of freedom. In my view—when it comes to government—there can be only one enduring kind: a republic governed by monarchists or a monarchy governed by republicans."

Heine is incapable of a dull paragraph. His prose, which fills eight volumes in a twelve-volume set of his major works in an American translation, scintillates with droll comparisons and fitful fancies: results of Heine's habitual scrutiny of accepted ideas, of men and events.

And there is Heine, the author of hauntingly beautiful German verse. The quintessential poet Heine is also "in." His *Book of Songs* made Heine famous before he was thirty years old. The book's fame soon spread worldwide as if the speech of the whole earth had never been confounded and the Tower of Babel had been destroyed in vain. Spokesman for all lovers, this poet voiced their feelings: the marvel, the joy, the anticipation—with a specialty in rejected love. In this small but crowded area, he had no equal in all of German Romantic literature. He, like no one else, knew where it hurt. He applied simple words to bind up the wound so that it would never heal, ever!, and his love lyrics will vie for permanence with the pangs of dispriz'd love:

> It is an old old story,
> But somehow stays quite new,
> And he who has just lived it—
> It breaks his heart in two.

But Heine was not only a love poet, and his poetry is now appreciated for a wider range of subjects than before. The venerable *Oxford Book of German Verse*, for instance, in its most recent edition, has broadened its Heine selection to include lesser known poems, among them "None will sing a Mass for me." To be sure: its opening lines are perennially adduced for their admonitory tone of self-incrimination, as a terrible warning to all would-be apostates. But the rest of the poem, with its pragmatic solicitude, is rarely cited. "When I lie buried," the poet advises his future widow,

"have a care for your feet and take a cab home after you
visit my grave."

Many know Heine as the author of the most famous
German ballad about the fisherman who came to grief in
his boat, on a rock in a bend of the river. Every child in
Germany learns the "Lorelei" and sings it to the tune by
Friedrich Silcher. Although Heine's books were burned by
the Nazis, there was no way of expunging this song from the
inward ears of generations. Its text appeared in an-
thologies, its author un-identified as "anonymous." But the
song was sung also in defiance. A class of school children in
World War II huddled in an air raid shelter during an
Allied bombing raid. When the sound of explosions pene-
trated concrete walls and a tight steel door, the teacher had
her anxious charges intone the "Lorelei." This story is
related by the sculptor Gert Gerresheim, himself one of
those children at the time, later the artificer of an im-
pressive memorial sculpture to Heine in Düsseldorf. (Two
of his prints, a linoleum cut and a woodcut, can be seen at
The Museum of Modern Art, New York.)

And there is Heine, the Jew, scorned for not being Jewish
enough and disdained for infusing everything he wrote with
his Jewishness. This Heine is receiving scrupulous and
salutary attention, not only in Germany: S.S. Prawer, Tay-
lor Professor of German Language and Literature, Univer-
sity of Oxford, has recently completed an exhaustive study,
Heine's Jewish Comedy, where he evaluates every single
Jew appearing in Heine's writings and all references to
Judaism.

But all the various facets of the variously perceived
writer pertain to one Heinrich Heine who bore the impress
of the time and the place of his birth.

The idea of Jewish emancipation conceived in the Ger-
many of Lessing and Mendelssohn began to become reality

in the 1790s. The impetus for civic equality came from the French Revolution, and the laws of the French occupation emancipated the Jews in the principalities of Western Germany in 1795. It was in this Western Germany that Heine was born on December 13, 1797, in Düsseldorf, on the banks of the Rhine, in the principality of Jülich-Berg, a city proud of its cultural activities and its gardens. Its Jewish community had been established in 1608, that is to say: it was a recent one and did not have a ghetto. The ancestors of Heine's mother had, as Court Jews, been financial advisers to the Duke of Jülich-Berg. From an intelligent and reasonably affluent family, Betty van Geldern sympathized with ideas of the French Revolution, and, in this age of enlightenment, took an interest in German literature.

Of limited financial means, Samson Heine, her fiancé, was at first unwelcome in the Düsseldorf Jewish community. The community as such had to pay taxes, and a newcomer not pulling his fiscal weight was considered a liability. But Betty successfully fought for his acceptance. A native of Bückeburg, near Hanover, Samson dealt in yard goods. Among his customers were the soldiers of Napoleon's army, who were outfitted in the wools imported by Samson Heine from England. As one leafs through the writings of Heinrich Heine, one is bound to notice the many references to different kinds of cloth which Heine knew by name. This manifest interest in his father's occupation bespeaks a serene relationship. He was a most affectionate son to his mother also, reporting to her only his triumphs.

Heine's most consistently controversial family relationship was with his uncle, Salomon Heine, a banker in Hamburg who helped him out with money again and again, finally settling a pension on him and later on Heine's widow. Understandably, Heine's dependence on his Uncle Salomon did not sit well with him. His letters to his uncle reel from requests for funds to defiant accusations and asseverations of loyalty. They make painful reading and bring home the realization that an "independent" poet pays a high price in pride. But when Heine opted for such an existence, moreover as a Jew, he already had an inkling of alternatives. What had he learned up to this point?

Seemingly peripheral, but fundamental for Heine, was a certain schoolroom. To supplement his general education in Düsseldorf, Heine, as a young child, attended a "religion school" run by a distant relative from Hamburg, one Hein Herz Rintelsohn. Here, Heine was taught some rudiments of Hebrew and, more significant for him, he was treated to biblical and rabbinic lore according well with his own propensities for fantasy. Heine—we may ask incredulously—, sat in a *cheder?* Did not a generation of Jews flee from all religion at the very thought of its narrowness? Heine's self-acceptance as a Jew was shaped here. For in place of an oppressive image of such a schoolroom, we should form one along the lines suggested by the historian Ismar Schorsch. Discussing Heine's contemporary, the painter Moritz Oppenheim, Schorsch urges that our understanding of early 19th-century German ideology be corrected with insights gained from social history. He points to the paintings of Oppenheim—who also portrayed Heine—as offering visual material for such a social history.

In particular, Oppenheim's oil painting "A Jewish School for Infants" reflects an ethos—precisely because it is not a naturalistic rendition but, more likely, an idealization. It conveys a sense of cheerfulness and orderliness, with touches of humor, as it depicts neatly dressed youngsters in a bright, clean schoolroom. A book from which a boy is reciting is not a pitiful tattered volume, but a carefully handled or recently acquired aid for teaching children the Hebrew alphabet: The letters are clear and almost the size of the pupil's hand resting on the page. Young expectations as idealized here tend not in the direction of pious self-pity, but towards well-being in a Jewish setting. We should imagine Heine receiving his early Hebrew instruction in Düsseldorf in this aura. It implanted a love for Judaism so deep that inevitable doubts, or anger with its practitioners did not dislodge it. An appetite for Jewish history seized Heine later.

But Heine's pragmatic family had other priorities, and after his stints at an elementary and a secondary school— from which he did not formally graduate—, he was expected to follow his father in commerce. He was sent to a trade school: this proved to be an unfortunate decision. He was sent to Frankfurt to be apprenticed in business: another unfortunate decision; to Hamburg for the same purpose and with the same result. And the family at last caught on that, no matter what, Heine was bent on a life devoted to intellectual pursuits. These abortive introductions to the world of commerce did, however, produce one unexpected result; it was during his very short sojourn in Frankfurt that he most probably had his first experience of a Jewish ghetto.

Having demonstrated that he was not suited for a career in business, Heine matriculated in 1819 at the University of Bonn as a student of law. He was more impressed by his contacts with August Wilhelm von Schlegel who lectured on the very unpragmatic subject of literature. In response to Schlegel's challenge that Lord Byron's poetry was untranslatable, Heine began to translate it. As Byron's grateful apprentice in Romanticism, Heine would, in 1851, call the third cycle of poems in his *Romancero* "Hebrew Melodies," after the master's collection.

The next and very brief stop in Heine's university career was Göttingen, from which he was expelled for duelling. But after he transferred to the University of Berlin in the summer of 1821, Heine's many and varied intellectual gifts

began to flourish. Literary circles opened to him in the
Berlin salon of Karl August and Rachel Varnhagen von
Ense, where he hobnobbed with the philosopher Georg
Wilhelm Friedrich Hegel and with the poets of the day—
Adalbert von Chamisso, Christian Dietrich Grabbe,
Willibald Alexis, among others. In this circle, he kept his
Jewishness to himself. But through the jurist Eduard Gans,
he made the acquaintance of the Association for the
Culture and Science of Judaism and its members, and he
became absorbed in the perusal of Jewish historical docu-
ments. While supposedly studying law, while travelling,
socializing and teaching, he indulged his writing, and pub-
lished Romantic poetry, satirical prose and two extraordi-
nary, but unsuccessful, verse plays.

But to give this dutiful recital of Heine's datable ac-
tivities—mentioning that he returned to Göttingen to com-
plete his studies, that he wandered on foot through the
Harz Mountains, that he visited Goethe in Weimar and
received his law degree with only a "pass" in July 1825—is
really to bypass what is less tangible but more determining
in the poet's development. Crucial was the emergence of his
uncompromising literary ambition, more powerful than his
reluctance to turn to Uncle Salomon for funds. Symp-
tomatic of an incipient talent for antagonizing his well-
wishers was his friendship with Moses Moser, a member of
the Association who sent him books and money, who lent
him his winter coat and was the patient recipient of Heine's
epistolary confidences. Heine would reproach him later,
from Paris: "Our friendship has not come to an end—it has
never existed." This aspect of Heine—the man as poet and
fickle friend—should also be part of even a thumbnail
biography.

As Heine faced his final examination for a law degree—in
which, *per se*, he had no interest—, he took a step which
has no satisfactory explanation. He travelled to nearby

Heiligenstadt where, on June 28, 1825, Pastor Gottlieb
Christian Grimm baptized him into the Protestant faith.
Heine regretted this step two months later and for the rest
of his life. His conversion was a purely pragmatic decision.
Upon the defeat of France, Prussian laws had reversed
many of the Jews' civic gains. Academic appointments were
expressly denied them, and Heine's stated expectation was
to receive such an appointment. He referred to his con-
version self-mockingly as his "entrance ticket to European
culture." He did not change his faith lightly: he had earlier
decried a friend's conversion to Christianity and had said
no to his parents when they discussed this possibility for
him. And yet, he took the step. And a fate as ironic as
Heine himself arranged that this entrance ticket would buy
him no admission after all. A teaching post in Berlin in the
field of law was denied him shortly after his conversion,
and a similar post in Munich in 1828. In 1830/31 a civil
service position in Hamburg eluded him.

Heine, meanwhile, wrote voluminously, and the pub-
lisher and bookseller Julius Campe, who met Heine in
January 1826, pounced on this new talent. In May 1826,
Campe published *Travel Pictures I*, which contained, in
addition to other prose and poetry, the *Harz Journey*, a
masterpiece. It had been previously serialized in a journal,
but had been blue-pencilled by an increasingly busy cen-
sor. Between them, Heine and his publisher resorted to
subterfuge to elude his heavy hand, but its weight was felt
for decades to come. And a fictitious friend was quoted by
Heine as having warned:

> My dear friend, you are a goner
> If you publish books of that kind.
> You should rather kow-tow humbly
> If you seek some wealth and honor.

I would never have advised you
Thus to speak before the people,
Thus to speak about the clergy
Or of those who ostracized you.

Nevertheless, the rate of Heine's publications accelerated. In April 1827, *Travel Pictures II* came out. Laden with social and political criticism, they bore little resemblance to previous vessels sailing under the travelogue flag. Heine practised prudence somewhat selectively, naming names in the book, but going sightseeing in England to wait out the expected storm over its appearance. Upon his return, his *Book of Songs* was published, and it made him famous. Cotta, the Munich publisher, offered him an editorial position which he took while hoping for other career prospects to materialize. He held this job for six months, then travelled widely to Italy, Austria, and the North Sea. His *Travel Pictures III* appeared in December 1829.

Heine's innermost strivings stand revealed through these bare bones of a biographical outline of his youth: come law, come sea, come livelihood, Heine had but one passion: writing. He confessed as much, in a Latin letter, to his university dean in Göttingen: how he had pursued the study of law for six years but had never intended jurisprudence to be his sole means of earning a living, how his main interest had been in the humanities. Today, we wonder how many other of his contemporaries, locked out by mystification and Latin, were privy to such a revelation. To most of his friends and to posterity, Heine fed a different story featuring conspiracies, malice, and legal discrimination. There is some truth to some of these postulates, but it is surely no less true that, as Sammons and others have suggested, Heine's pursuit of his professed career may have lacked both vigor and conviction.

We may also wonder if Heine would relish everything

that his repute has wrought today. Undoubtedly, he would be gratified by the new editions of his works and would, if he could, buy his wife a new shawl. On the other hand, historical research is scraping the patina from his life story—some of which he himself had applied. Just as today's besieged celebrities take refuge behind tall tales to avoid the dullness of their provenance or embarrassing disclosures, so Heine created a persona in autobiographical remarks strewn throughout various works. He was rumored to have threatened family members to "tell all" in his *Memoirs*, unless. . . . And whether or not this was so, we can be sure that the *Memoirs*, published posthumously, pulsate with life, but are fatal if swallowed as factual information.

Two reasons, meanwhile, induced the real Heinrich Heine to decide to leave for France, a move he had contemplated for three years. One reason arrived in packages on his doorstep on the North Frisian island of Helgoland, namely news of the French July Revolution of 1830. He welcomed it in identifiably Heinesque style: "Sun rays wrapped in newspaper, setting my soul aflame to a point of wildest conflagration. I felt as if I could set the whole ocean on fire as far as the North Pole, with the glow of my enthusiasm and the wild joy blazing inside me. Now I know why the sea smelled of cake. The River Seine had spread the good news directly into the sea and the beautiful water sprites [. . .] gave a *thé dansant* in celebration of the big event, and that's why the whole sea smelled of cake. I ran through the house like mad and kissed first the roundly hostess and then her friendly seawolf; and I also embraced the Prussian Commissary for Justice."

And Heine left shortly after the Berlin censor provided the second reason for leaving Germany by interdicting and confiscating his *Travel Pictures IV.*

He travelled to Paris via Frankfurt, where he stopped to

have his portrait painted by Moritz Oppenheim, and two days after arriving in Paris, he made the German-French connection by inspecting a famous Middle High German illuminated manuscript in the *Bibliothèque Royale*. Many other Germans of his generation loved France for its ideals of liberty, but Heine had also more personal reasons. As a youngster, he had had a glimpse of Napoleon during the French emperor's visit to Düsseldorf in 1811, and his memory of the perceived bestower of liberty to the Rhineland assumed a life of its own as the years went by. Furthermore, those born in Düsseldorf during the French occupation were given the right to live in France: Heine had reason to feel at home. He said he felt like a fish in water in Paris— "No; if one fish were to enquire after another, it would reply, 'I feel like Heine in Paris!'" And if we recall, as seems appropriate, a previous piscine comparison by Heine, to the effect that Germanness was to him what water was to a fish, then we should not be tempted to estimate Heine's love of successive domiciles, but rather be content merely to conclude that utmost well-being invariably reminded Heine of fish, regardless which side of the Rhine.

Heine was welcomed in Paris by the *literati*, among them Honoré de Balzac, Victor Hugo, George Sand, Alfred de Musset, Alexandre Dumas, and by musicians like Luigi Cherubini, Frédéric Chopin—to drop only the best known names. Baron de Rothschild's reception of Heine was characterized by the poet as "quite famillionair," a neologism destined to enter the annals of psychoanalytic literature via Freud's *Wit and its Relation to the Unconscious*.

Heine now acted as correspondent for German newspapers—he had contributed to no fewer than fifty by the end of his life. He pioneered, together with Ludwig Börne, a journalistic prose previously unknown in Germany, the *feuilleton*. "Leaves" from Börne and Heine wafted to German readers the aromas of an exciting, stimulating, and threatening city, in a witty style blending report and commentary.

For most of his life, Heine suffered ill health. Although his illness was for a long time thought to have been syphilis—it affected his eyes and eventually his spine and limbs—, more recent medical knowledge has diagnosed it as myatrophic lateral sclerosis. Heine spent his last eight years confined to bed, in his "mattress grave."

It is at this time that Heine is said to have returned to Judaism. He countered: "I have not returned to Judaism because I never left it," and he confused the issue further by shifting his tongue from one cheek to the other: "You have no idea how much pain I am suffering," he wrote to a friend in 1850, "and it is a miracle that I've not become completely stupefied by it. And there's no hope for improvement, only the comfortless recognition that this agonizing disease might, towards its end, become even more horrible. [. . .] Thank God that I have a God again so that I can, in the excess of pain, permit myself a few cursing blasphemies; an atheist is denied such relief." In many of his writings, Heine had addressed the good Lord with a familiarity adjoining blasphemy on one side and old friendship on the other. An early letter to Moser argued: "It is very ill-behaved of our good Lord to plague me now with such pain. It is, moreover, unpolitic of the old gentleman because He knows that I want to do so much for Him. Or has the old Baron of Sinai and sole ruler of Judea also experienced Enlightenment, put aside His nationality, abandoned His claims and followers in exchange for a few vague, cosmopolitan ideas? I'm afraid the old gentleman has lost His head, and *le petit juif d'Amsterdam* [Spinoza] may with justification whisper into His ear: '*Entre nous, Monsieur, vous n'existez pas.*' And what of us? do we exist? For heaven's sake, don't tell me again that I am only an idea!" Or, five years later, when Heine made the point that many of the world's sorrows are due to lack of money: "You may well be right, the good Lord was strapped for funds when He created the world. He had to borrow money for the enterprise from the devil and mortgage the world to him as security."

Heine's mixture of good humor, bright intelligence, and not exclusively respectful thoughts of a very close God appears to be in a modern mode, but also is reminiscent of such Jewish reliables as Abraham, who argued with God, or Rabbi Levi Yitzhak of Berditchev, who downright accused God at times.

Yet Heine was never in any way religiously observant. For years, he derided the pernicious effect of all religion, including Judaism. For a time he lined up Judaism with German ideology because both aspired to morality; or he would view a virile Judaism in contrast to a sickly, hypocritical Christianity:

> Our God, he did not perish
> As a sorry mamby-pamby
> For mankind, he did not cherish
> Philanthroplets, blabberjacks.

So argues the rabbi in Heine's poem "Disputation."

Heine's ideas on Judaism swayed together with his other ideas. Ever since his student days, Heine had struggled with the meaning of Jewishness in 19th-century Western Europe. His search for a meaningful Judaism may have been one reason why, in Berlin, he had joined the Association for the Culture and Science of Judaism. Its members sought to make Judaism intellectually respectable by subjecting it to Western methods of enquiry. Under the roof of the Association, Heine taught three history lessons per week, and held French and German classes for young Jews, many of whom had come to Berlin from the Eastern provinces, hoping for greater freedom. Whereas the Association folded for lack of broad appeal and, consequently, for lack of funds, its aims survived. The impact of Heine's friendship with its leading members was to add a meaningful dimension to his previous experience of Judaism. The lessons from his religion-school room he had clearly outgrown; routine adult studies were pursued in assemblies he did not seek out. It was the intellectually élitist emphasis given to Judaism by the Association which was compatible with Heine's broader literary interests. He saw no ideological conflict between Jewishness and Germanness. Critically, laughingly, he contended with both.

Heine was, for instance, fascinated by Jewish historical studies. The Middle Ages specifically, which had played so evocative a role in the then current literary Romanticism, came to mean, for Heine, medieval Jewish communities and their persecutions, especially along the familiar Rhine. He conceived the idea of writing a Jewish historical narrative work modelled after Sir Walter Scott.

Thus, *The Rabbi of Bacherach* came to be. Heine worked on the historical research with enthusiasm, but the actual writing of the piece—first intended as a novella, then as a novel—became more and more desultory, was interrupted by his writing of the *Harz Journey* and then abandoned. He finished only Part I and possibly sketches for Part II, but actually wrote Parts II and III about fifteen years later, in 1840.

This was the year of the anti-semitic Damascus riots. A monk had been found murdered in Damascus, and the Jews of that city were accused of ritual murder. Among Western European Jews, agitated by this event, was Heine. He remembered his unfinished early work which had a ritual murder accusation in it, and returned to it.

Readers cannot fail to notice how the chapters of the fragment differ from one another in tone, how the beginning of Part II does not dovetail with the end of Part I; how Part III is quixotic, introducing a dashing Romantic hero, a convert to Christianity who is strangely affecting. The disjointed composition of the work accounts for the lack of narrative smoothness. The fragment is not so much a failed novel but, like virtually all of Heine's passionate prose, a response to reality, albeit in historical garb. Its end is upbeat: a whole new development promises to coincide with the start of a festive lunch.

In no other work has Heine permitted his love for Judaism to show as it does here in the details of the domestic Passover celebration and of the synagogue service, from the vantage point of the women's gallery, at that. Max Liebermann's illustrations first appeared in 1923 in a limited bibliophile edition. With their unsentimental exactitude, they harmonize to perfection with the mood of Heine's narrative.

The other prose piece printed in this edition, "Shylock," has been excerpted from Heine's *Shakespeare's Maidens and Women* (1838) where it is entitled "Jessica." It represents a first "defense" of Judaism in economic, not theological terms. Frederic Ewen's translation was chosen because it keeps the crisp, polemical tone of the original.

In consonance with Heine's conviction that Jewishness was not to be seen in isolation, but that an enlightened Europe would lead to Jewish equality, he incorporated Jewish themes into many of his writings. *The Rabbi of Bacherach* and "Shylock" with their specifically Jewish subject matter thus are exceptional and stand as Masterworks of Modern Jewish Writing.

The translation of "Hebrew Melodies," the third cycle of poems in *Romancero*, is by Hal Draper. It leaves nothing to be desired. His *The Complete Poems of Heinrich Heine. A Modern English Version* is the result of skillful labor over a period of more than thirty years.

The "Hebrew Melodies" were immediately popular, and were often translated into Hebrew, although "Dame Care" was probably the first to be translated by Selig Allerhand in *Kochbc Yitzhak* (1852). Nathan Samuel translated one of Heine's early Dream poems (Lemberg 1868). "Disputation" from "Hebrew Melodies" appeared in *Zimrath Ha-aretz* in 1872 in a Hebrew version by David Wechsler, "Yehudah Ha-Levy" from the same cycle in Warsaw, 1886. From that time on, Heine's poetry and prose were frequently rendered by Hebrew poets and translators.

Heine's writings have been highly praised in English-speaking countries, especially by established writers. Among the earliest was George Eliot whose essay "German Wit: Heinrich Heine" (1856) celebrated Heine as an exception to teutonic dreariness. Heine figures in a gallery of *Jewish Portraits* by the Victorian author Katie (Lady) Magnus, and he inspired Israel Zangwill to put together what we could call a literary collage, interspersing translated passages from Heine's prose with his own links for a chapter in his *Dreamers of the Ghetto* (1892).

In America, Emma Lazarus translated some 43 poems by Heine into superb *Poems and Ballads*. Mark Twain, who said of himself that he could understand German as well as the maniac who invented it but could "talk" it best through an interpreter, tried his hand at rendering the "Lorelei" into English. From the result it is clear that the delight he took in the incomprehensibility of the German language outstripped his skill in translating it by the length of a Mississippi steam boat. Any entries for first prize in an English "Lorelei" category would be strongly contested by James Thomson ("B.V.") whose truly poetic 1892 rendition succeeds in transmitting both meaning and mood of the original.

In the writing of Heine, as in other writers of significance, the style is the man. What a translation of Heine would aim to convey is the particular quality of his style, which is all verve. I have chosen Charles Godfrey Leland's translation of *The Rabbi of Bacherach* because it most adequately captures the essence of Heine's prose rhythm. I have adjusted his vocabulary in two main directions: a few extra "Sad's" and "Dark's," gratuitous gifts from the translator, have been removed so that Heine's original can shine in its own coloration, and the appurtenances of the ritual services are given the names customary in Jewish usage. All translations in the Introduction are mine.

For their helpful suggestions I thank Professors Jerry Glenn and Hugh B. Staples, University of Cincinnati.

Elizabeth Petuchowski
Cincinnati
January 1987

Old Bacharach

The Rabbi of Bacherach

A FRAGMENT

BY HEINRICH HEINE

Translated into English by Charles Godfrey Leland (1906)

Updated by Elizabeth Petuchowski (1987)

FIRST CHAPTER

Below the mountainous range known as the Rheingau, the banks of the Rhine river put off their smiling look. Where the hills and cliffs with their romantic castles rise more defiantly, and where a wilder, sterner dignity prevails, there lies, like a fearful legend of olden times, the gloomy and ancient town of Bacherach. But these walls with their toothless battlements and eyeless turrets, in whose nooks and niches the winds blow and the sparrows nest, were not always so decayed and ruinous, and in these poverty-stricken, repulsive mud lanes which one sees through the torn gate, there did not always reign that dreary silence which is only now and then broken by crying children, scolding women, and lowing cows. These walls were once proud and strong, and these lanes were alive with a fresh, free life, power and pomp, joy and sorrow, much love and much hate. For Bacherach of old belonged to those municipalities which were founded by the Romans during their rule on the Rhine; and its inhabitants, though the times which came after were very stormy, and though they fell first under the Hohenstaufen, and then under the Wittelsbach rule, managed, after the example of the other cities on the Rhine, to maintain a tolerably free communal life. This consisted of an alliance of different social elements, in which the patricians and those of the guilds which were subdivided according to their different trades, severally strove for sole power, so that while they were bound to keep a united front against the robber-barons, they, never-

21

theless, persisted in domestic dissentions waged for conflicting interests, the results of which were constant feuds, little social intercourse, much mistrust, and not seldom actual outbursts of violence. The bailiff sat in the high tower of Sareck, and swooped downwards like his falcon, whenever called for, also many a time uncalled. The clergy ruled in the dark through spiritual darkness. One of the most isolated and helpless of bodies, gradually elbowed out of all rights was the little Jewish community. This was first formed in Bacherach in the days of the Romans, and during the later persecution of Jews it had taken in many a flock of fugitive co-religionists.

The great persecution of the Jews began with the crusades, and raged most furiously about the middle of the fourteenth century, at the end of the great pestilence, which was, like all other great public disasters, attributed to the Jews, because people declared that they had drawn down the wrath of God, and with the help of the lepers had poisoned the wells. The enraged populace, especially the hordes of Flagellants: half naked men and women, who, lashing themselves for penance and singing a mad hymn to the Virgin, swept over South Germany and the Rhenish provinces, murdered in those days many thousand Jews, torturing others, or baptizing them by force. There was another accusation which had come down from earlier times, and which through all the Middle Ages, even to the beginning of the last century, cost much blood and suffering. This was the ridiculous story, often repeated in chronicle and legend, that the Jews stole the consecrated wafer, and stabbed it through with knives till blood ran from it. And to this it was added that at the feast of the Passover the Jews slew Christian children to use their blood in the midnight service.

Therefore on this festival the Jews, sufficiently hated for their religion, their wealth, and the debts due to them, were entirely in the hands of their enemies, who could easily bring about their destruction by spreading the report of such a child-murder, perhaps even secretly putting a bloody infant's corpse in the house of a Jew thus accused. Then there would be an attack by night on the Jews at their prayers, where there was murder, plunder, and baptism; and great miracles wrought by the dead child aforesaid, whom the Church eventually canonised. Saint Werner is one of these holy beings, and in his honour the magnificent abbey of Oberwesel was founded. It is now one of the most beautiful ruins on the Rhine, and which, with the Gothic grandeur of its long, lancet windows, proudly aspiring pillars, and marvellous stone-carving, so strangely enchants us when we wander by it on some merry green summer's day, and do not know what was its origin. In honour of this saint three other great churches were built on the Rhine, and innumerable Jews murdered or maltreated. All this happened in the year 1287; and in Bacherach, where one of these Saint Werner's churches stood, the Jews suffered much misery and persecution. However, for two centuries after, they were spared such attacks of popular rage, though they were continually subject to enmity and threatening.

Yet the more hate oppressed them from without, the more earnestly and tenderly did the Jews of Bacherach cherish their domestic life within, and the deeper was the growth among them of piety and the fear of God. The ideal exemplar of a life given to God was seen in their local Rabbi Abraham, who, though as yet a young man, was famed far and wide for his learning. Born in Bacherach, his father, who had been the rabbi there before him, had charged him in his last will to follow him in office and never to leave the place unless for fear of life. This command, and a cabinet full of rare books, was all which his parent, who lived in poverty and learning, left him. However, Rabbi Abraham was a very rich man, for he had married the only daughter of his paternal uncle, who had been a dealer in jewellery, and whose great fortunes he had inherited. A few mischief-makers in the community hinted now and then that the rabbi had married only for money. But the women one and all denied this, declaring it was a well-known story that the rabbi, long ere he went to Spain, was in love with "Beautiful Sara," and how she waited for him seven years till he returned; he having already wedded her against the will of her father, and even her own inclination, by the betrothal-ring. For every Jew can make a Jewish girl his lawful wife, if he can put a ring on her finger, and say at the same time: "I take thee for my wife, according to the law of Moses and Israel." And when Spain was mentioned, the same gossips were wont to smile in the same significant manner, and all because of an obscure rumour that, though Rabbi Abraham had studied the holy law industriously enough at the high school of Toledo, yet that he had imitated Christian customs and become imbued with habits of free thinking, like many Spanish Jews who had at that time attained a very remarkable degree of culture.

And yet in their hearts the tale-bearers put no faith in these reports; for ever since his return from Spain the daily life of the Rabbi had been to the last degree pure, pious, and earnest. He carried out the least details of all religious customs and ceremonies with anxious conscientiousness; he fasted every Monday and Thursday—only on Sabbaths and feast days did he indulge in meat or wine; his time was passed in prayer and study; by day he taught the Law to the students, whom his fame had drawn to Bacherach, and by night he gazed on the stars in heaven, or into the eyes of the Beautiful Sara. His marriage was childless, yet there was no lack of life or gaiety in the household. The great hall in his home, which stood next to the synagogue, was open to the whole community, so that people went and came from it

without ceremony, some offering short prayers, others ex-
changing news, or taking mutual counsel when in trouble.
Here the children played on Sabbath mornings while the
weekly "portion" was read; here many met for wedding or
funeral processions, and quarrelled or were reconciled;
here, too, those who were cold found a warm stove, and the
hungry a well-spread table. And, moreover, the Rabbi had
a multitude of relations, brothers and sisters, with their
wives and children, as well as an endless array of uncles
and cousins, his and his wife's, all of whom looked up to the
Rabbi as the head of the family, and so made themselves at
home in his house, early and late, and never failed to dine
with him on all great festivals. Special among these grand
gatherings in the Rabbi's house was the annual celebration
of the Passover, a very ancient and remarkable feast which
Jews still hold every year in the month Nissen, in eternal
remembrance of their deliverance from Egyptian captivity.

Which takes place as follows: As soon as it is dark the
matron of the family lights the lamps, spreads the table-
cloth, places in its midst three pieces of flat, unleavened
bread, covers them with a napkin, and places on the raised
area six little dishes containing symbolical food, that is, an
egg, lettuce, horse-radish, the bone of a lamb, and a brown
mixture of raisins, cinnamon, and nuts. At this table the
father of the family sits among relations and friends, and
reads to them from a very curious book called the *Agade*,
whose contents are a strange mixture of legends of their
forefathers, wondrous tales of Egypt, remarkable stories,
questions of theology, prayers and festival songs. During
this celebration there is a grand supper, and even during
the reading there is tasting of the symbolical food and
nibbling of matzos, while four cups of red wine are drunk.
Mournfully merry, seriously playful, and mysteriously se-
cret is the character of this nocturnal festival, and the
usual traditional singing intonation with which the *Agade* is

read by the father, and now and then re-echoed in chorus by the hearers, at one time thrills the inmost soul as with a shudder, anon calms it as if it were a mother's lullaby, and anon startles it so suddenly into waking that even those Jews who have long fallen away from the faith of their fathers and run after gentile joys and honours, are moved to their very hearts when by chance the old well-known tones of the Passover songs ring in their ears.

And so Rabbi Abraham once sat in his great hall surrounded by relations, disciples, and many other guests, to celebrate the great feast of the Passover. All around was unusually brilliant; over the table hung the gaily embroidered silk table cloth, whose gold fringes touched the floor; the plate with the symbolic food shone in a pleasing way, as did the tall wine-filled goblets, adorned with embossed images of holy legends. The men sat in their black cloaks and black broad-brimmed hats, with white collars; the women, in wonderful glittering garments of Lombard stuffs, wore on their heads and necks ornaments of gold and pearls, and the silver Sabbath lamp poured forth its pleasant light on the pleased faces of parents and children, happy in their piety. On the purple velvet cushions of a chair, higher than the others, and reclining as the Law enjoins, sat Rabbi Abraham, and read and sang the *Agade*, while the mixed assembly joined with him, or answered in the appointed places. The Rabbi also wore the appointed black festival garment, his nobly-formed but somewhat severe features wore a milder expression than usual, his lips smiled in the dark-brown beard as if they would fain tell something agreeable, while in his eyes there was an expression as of happy remembrances and anticipation. The Beautiful Sara, who sat at his side on a similarly high velvet cushion, wore, as hostess, none of her ornaments—only white linen enveloped her slender form and good and

27

gentle face. This face was touchingly beautiful, even as the beauty of Jewish women is generally of a peculiarly moving kind; for the consciousness of the deep misery, the bitter scorn, and the evil events amid which her kindred and friends dwelt, gave to her lovely features a sorrowful intensity and an ever-watchful apprehension out of a love that most deeply touches our hearts. So on this evening the fair Sara sat looking at the eyes of her husband, yet glancing also at the beautiful parchment book of the *Agade* which lay before her, bound in gold and velvet. It was an old heirloom, with ancient wine stains on it, which had come down from the days of her grandfather, and in which were many boldly and brightly-coloured pictures, which she had often as a little girl looked at so eagerly on Passover evenings, and which represented all kinds of Bible stories— how Abraham smashes with a hammer the stone idols of his father, how the angels come to him, how Moses slays the Mitzri, how Pharaoh sits in state on his throne, how the frogs give him no peace even at table, how he—thank God!—is drowned, how the children of Israel go cautiously through the Red Sea; how they stand open-mouthed, with their sheep, cows, and oxen, before Mount Sinai; how pious King David plays the harp; and, finally, how Jerusalem, with the towers and battlements of its temple, shines in the splendor of the sun.

The second wine-cup had been served, the faces and voices of the guests grew brighter and the Rabbi, as he took a piece of unleavened bread and raised it high, happily presenting it, read these words from the *Agade:* "See! This is the food which our fathers ate in Egypt! Let every one who is hungry come and eat! Let every one who is needy come and share the joys of our Passover! This year we celebrate it here, but next year, in the land of Israel. This year we celebrate it in servitude, but in the year to come as sons of freedom!"

Just then the hall-door opened, and there entered two tall, pale men, wrapped in very broad cloaks, who said: "Peace be with you. We are fellow Jews on a journey, and wish to share the Passover-feast with you!" And the Rabbi replied promptly and kindly: "Peace be with you, sit ye down near me!" The two strangers sat down at the table and the Rabbi read on. While the company were still repeating after him, he would address a pleasant, loving word to his wife; and playing on the old saying that on this evening a Jewish father of a family regards himself as a king, said to her, "Rejoice, oh my Queen!" But she replied, smiling sadly, "The Prince is wanting," meaning by that a son, who as a passage in the *Agade* requires, shall ask his father, with a set formula of words, for the meaning of the festival. The Rabbi said nothing, but only pointed with his finger to a picture on the opened leaves of the *Agade*. It was drawn, showing how most beautifully the three angels came to Abraham, announcing that he would have a son by his wife Sara, who, out of curiosity, meanwhile, is listening with feminine pertness from behind the tent-door. This little sign caused a threefold blush to rise to the cheeks of Beautiful Sara, who looked down, and then glanced pleasantly at her husband. He went on chanting the wonderful story how Rabbi Jesua, Rabbi Eliezer, Rabbi Asaria, Rabbi Akiba, and Rabbi Tarphen sat reclining in the Bona-Brak, and conversed all night long of the Exodus of the children of Israel from Egypt till their disciples came to tell them it was daylight, and that the great morning prayer was already being read in the synagogue.

As Beautiful Sara listened with devotion while constantly looking at her husband, she saw that in an instant his face contorted horribly, his cheeks and lips were deadly pale, and his eyes glared like icicles; but almost immediately his features became calm and cheerful as before, his cheeks and lips grew ruddy, he looked about him gaily—nay, it seemed as if a wild mood, such as was foreign to his nature, had seized him. Beautiful Sara was frightened as she had never been in all her life, and a cold shudder came over her—less from the momentary manifestation of dumb horror which she had seen in her husband's face, than from the joyousness which followed it and turned to rollicking jollity. The Rabbi cocked his cap comically, first on one ear, then on the other, pulled and twisted his beard into funny shapes, sang the *Agade* texts like tavern songs; and in the enumeration of the Egyptian plagues, where it is customary to dip the forefinger in the full wine-cup and cast the adhering drops to the earth, he sprinkled the young girls near him with the red wine, and there was great wailing over ruined ruffles, and ringing laughter. At every instant Beautiful Sara became more uneasy at this convulsive merriment of her husband, and oppressed with nameless fears, she gazed on the buzzing swarm of variously illuminated guests who comfortably rocked to and fro, nibbling the thin Passover bread, drinking wine, gossiping, or singing aloud, full of joy.

Then came the time for supper. All rose to wash, and beautiful Sara brought the great silver basin, richly adorned with embossed gold figures, which she presented to every guest, while water was poured over his hands. As she held it for the Rabbi, he gave her a significant look, and quietly slipped out of the door. In obedience to the sign Beautiful Sara followed him, when he grasped her hand, and in the greatest haste hurried her through the dark lanes of Bacherach, out of the city gate to the highway which leads to Bingen along the Rhine.

It was one of those nights in spring which are indeed softly warm and starry withal, yet inspire the soul with strange uncanny feelings. There was something deathly in the fragrance of the flowers, the birds sang peevishly and anxiously, the moon cast spiteful yellow stripes of light over

31

the dark stream as it went murmuring, the lofty masses of the Rhine cliffs looked dimly like menacingly quivering giants' heads, the watchman on the tower of Castle Strahleck blew a melancholy tune, and with it rang in jarring rivalry the funeral bell of Saint Werner's. Beautiful Sara carried the silver ewer in her right hand, while the Rabbi grasped her left, and she felt that his fingers were ice-cold, and that his arm trembled; but still she went on with him in silence, perhaps because she was accustomed to obey blindly and unquestioning—perhaps, too, because her lips were mute with fear and anxiety.

Below Castle Sonneck, opposite Lorch, about the place where the hamlet of Nieder Rheinbach now stands, there rises a cliff which arches out over the Rhine bank. The Rabbi ascended it with his wife, looked around on every side, and gazed on the stars. Trembling and shivering, as with the fears of death, Beautiful Sara looked at his pale face, which seemed spectre-like in the moon-rays, and seemed to express by turns pain, terror, piety, and rage. But when the Rabbi suddenly snatched from her hands the silver ewer and threw it clattering into the Rhine, she could no longer endure her agony of uncertainty, and crying out, "*Schadai*, full of mercy!" threw herself at his feet, and implored him to reveal the dark enigma.

Unable at first to speak, the Rabbi moved his lips without uttering a sound, till at last he cried, "Do you see the Angel of Death? There below he sweeps over Bacherach. But we have escaped his sword. Praised be God!" And in a voice still trembling with horror, he told her that while he was happily reclining and singing the *Agade* he glanced by chance under the table, and saw at his feet the bloody corpse of a little child. "Then I knew," continued the Rabbi, "that our two late-coming guests were not of the community of Israel, but of the assembly of the godless, who had plotted to bring that corpse stealthily into the

33

house so as to accuse us of child-murder, and stir up the people to plunder and murder us. Had I given a sign that I saw through that work of darkness I should simply have brought destruction on the instant to me and mine, and only by craft did I preserve our lives. Praised be God! Grieve not, Beautiful Sara. Our relations and friends will also be saved. It was only my blood which the wretches wanted. I have escaped them, and they will be satisfied with my silver and gold. Come with me, Beautiful Sara, to another land. We will leave misfortune behind us, and that it may not follow us I have thrown to it the silver ewer, the last of my possessions, as reconciliation. The God of our fathers will not forsake us. Come down, you are weary. There is Silent Wilhelm standing by his boat; he will row us up the Rhine."

Speechless, and as if every limb was broken, Beautiful Sara lay in the arms of the Rabbi, who slowly bore her down to the river bank. There stood Wilhelm, a deaf and dumb youth, but yet beautiful as a picture, who, to maintain his old fostermother, who was a neighbour of the Rabbi, was a fisherman, and kept his boat in this place. It seemed as if he had divined the intention of Abraham, and was waiting for him, for on his silent lips there was an expression as of sweet sympathy and pity, and his great blue eyes rested as with deep meaning on Beautiful Sara, while he lifted her carefully into the canoe.

The glance of the silent youth roused Beautiful Sara from her stupefaction, and she realised at once that all which her husband had told her was no mere dream, and a stream of bitter tears poured over her cheeks, which now were as white as her garment. So she sat in the middle of the canoe, a weeping image of white marble, while by her sat her husband and Silent Wilhelm, who was eagerly rowing.

Whether it was owing to the measured beat of the oars,

or the rocking of the boat, or the fresh perfume from the Rhine banks whereon joy grows, it ever happens that even the most sorrowful being is marvellously calmed when on a night in spring he is lightly borne in a light canoe on the dear, clear Rhine stream. For in truth old, kind-hearted Father Rhine cannot bear that his children shall weep, so, calming their crying, he rocks them on his trusty arm, and tells them his most beautiful stories, and promises them his most golden treasures, perhaps even the ancient long-sunk Nibelungen hoard. Little by little the tears of Beautiful Sara ceased to flow; her worst sorrow seemed to be washed away by the eddying, whispering waves, the night lost its sinister horror, while her native hills bade her the tenderest farewell. Most reassuringly of all did her favourite mountain, the Kedrich, give her a farewell greeting; and it seemed as if far up in the strange moonlight, resting on its summit, she saw a lady with outstretched arms, while the daring dwarfs swarmed out of their clefts in the rocks, and a rider came rushing up the rocks in full gallop. And Beautiful Sara felt as if she were a child again, sitting once more in the lap of her aunt from Lorch, who was telling her the brave tale of the bold knight who freed the stolen damsel from the dwarfs, and many other true stories of the wonderful Wisperthal "over there," where the birds talk as sensibly as any mortals, and of Gingerbread Land, where good, obedient children go, and of enchanted princesses, singing trees, crystal castles, golden bridges, laughing water-sprites. . . . But all at once among these pleasant tales which began to send forth sounds of music and to gleam with lovely light, Beautiful Sara heard the voice of her father, who scolded the poor aunt for putting such nonsense into the child's head. Then it seemed to her as if they set her on the little stool before her father's velvet-covered chair, who with a soft hand stroked her long hair, and smiled as if well pleased, and rocked himself comfortably in his full Sabbath dressing-gown of blue silk. Yes, it must be the Sabbath, for the flowered cover was spread on the table, all the utensils in the room shone polished like looking-glasses, the white-bearded beadle sat beside her father, and ate raisins and talked in Hebrew; even little Abraham came in with a very large book, and modestly begged leave of his uncle to expound a portion of the Holy Scripture, that he might prove that he had learned much during the past week, and therefore deserved much praise—and a corresponding quantity of cakes. . . . Then the little lad laid the book on the broad arm of the chair, and explained the history of Jacob and Rachel, and how Jacob lifted up his voice and wept when he first saw his little cousin Rachel, how he talked so confidingly with her by the well, how he had to serve seven years for her, and how speedily they passed away for him, and how he at last married and loved her for ever and ever. . . . Then all at once Beautiful Sara remembered how her father cried with merry voice, "Will you not, like that also, marry cousin Sara?" To which little Abraham seriously replied, "That I will, and she shall wait seven years too." These memories stole like twilight shadows through the soul of the beautiful wife, and she saw how she and her little cousin—now so great a man and her husband—played like children together in the leafy tabernacle; how they were delighted with the colorful carpets, flowers, mirrors, and gilded apples; how little Abraham talked with her more tenderly, till he grew to be larger and less amiable, and at last of full growth and altogether grim. . . . And now she sits in her room alone of a Saturday evening; the moon shines brightly through the window, and the door flies open, and cousin Abraham, in travelling garb and pale as death, comes in, and grasps her hand and puts a gold ring on her finger, and says solemnly, "I hereby take you to be my wife, according to the laws of God and of Israel." "But now," he added,

with a trembling voice, "now I must go to Spain. Farewell—
for seven years you must wait for me." So he hurried away,
and Sara, weeping, told the tale to her father, who roared
and raged. "Cut off your hair, for now you are a married
woman," and he rode after Abraham to compel him to give
her a letter of divorcement; but he was over the hills and
far away, and the father returned silently to his house. And
when Beautiful Sara helped to draw off his boots, and to
soothe him said that Abraham would return in seven years,
he cursed and cried, "Seven years shall you go begging,"
and he soon died.

And so old memories chased each other through her
brain like a hurried play of shadows, the images intermix-
ing and blending strangely, while between them went and
came half-known and unknown bearded faces, and great
flowers with marvellous broad spreading foliage. Then the
Rhine seemed to murmur the melodies of the *Agade*, and
from its waters the pictures, large as life and in strange
exaggerated guise, came forth one by one. There was the
forefather Abraham painfully and hurriedly breaking the
idols, who were hastily putting themselves back together;
the Mitzri defending himself fiercely against the angry
Moses; Mount Sinai flashing and flaming; King Pharaoh
swimming in the Red Sea, holding his zigzagged gold crown
tight in his teeth, frogs with men's faces swimming behind
him, and the waves foaming and roaring, while a dark
giant-hand rises threatening from the deep.

That was the Mouse Tower of Bishop Hatto, and the
canoe shot through the Binger Eddy. By this Beautiful Sara
was somewhat aroused from her dreams. She gazed at the
hills on the shore, from whose summits the castle lights
gleamed, and at whose feet the mists shimmering in moon-
rays began to rise. Suddenly she seemed to see there her
friends and relations, as they, with corpse-like faces and
flowing shrouds, passed in awful procession along the

Rhine. . . . All grew dark before her eyes, an icy current
ran through her soul, and, as if in sleep, she only heard the
Rabbi recite the night-prayer for her slowly and painfully,
as if at a deathbed, and dreamily she stammered the words,
"Ten thousand to the right, ten thousand to the left, to
protect the king from the terrors of the night."

Then all at once the oppressive gloom and darkness
passed away, the sombre curtain was torn from heaven, and
there appeared, far above, the holy city Jerusalem, with its
towers and gates; the Temple gleamed in golden splendour,
and in its fore-court Sara saw her father in his yellow
Sabbath dressing-gown, smiling as if well pleased. All her
friends and relations looked out from the round windows of
the Temple, merrily greeting her; in the Holy of Holies
knelt pious King David, in his purple mantle and golden
crown; sweetly rang his song and the tone from his harp,
and smiling happily Beautiful Sara fell asleep.

SECOND CHAPTER

As Beautiful Sara opened her eyes they were almost dazzled by the rays of the sun. The high towers of a great city rose before her, and Silent Wilhelm with his boat-hook stood upright in the canoe, and pushed and guided it through the lively crowding of many vessels, gay with pennons and streamers, whose crews either looked leisurely at passers-by or were in groups busied in loading with chests, bales, and casks the lighters which should bear them to the shore, and with it all was a deafening noise, the constant halloh cry of steersmen, the calling of traders from the shore, and the scolding of the custom-house officials who, in their red coats with white maces and white faces, jumped from boat to boat.

"Yes, Beautiful Sara," said the Rabbi, cheerfully smiling to his wife, "this is the world famous, free, imperial, and commercial city of Frankfurt-on-the-Main, and we are now travelling on that Main river. Do you see those pleasant-looking houses up there, surrounded by green hillocks? That is Sachsenhausen, from which our lame Gumpertz brings us the fine myrrh for the Feast of the Tabernacles. Here you see the strong Main River Bridge, with thirteen arches, over which many men, waggons, and horses safely pass, and in the middle stands a little house of which Aunt Birdy says that a baptized Jew lives there, who pays six farthings to every man who brings him a dead rat on account of the Jewish community, who are obliged to deliver annually to the city council five thousand rats' tails for tribute."

At the thought of this war, which the Frankfurt Jews were obliged to keep up with the rats, Beautiful Sara burst out laughing. The bright sunlight, and the new colourful world now before her, had driven all the terrors and horrors of the past night from her soul, and as she was lifted to land from the canoe by Silent Wilhelm and her husband, she felt permeated as with a sense of joyful safety. But Silent Wilhelm looked long with his beautiful deep blue eyes into her face, half sadly, half cheerfully, and then with a significant glance at the Rabbi, sprang back into his boat and disappeared.

"Silent Wilhelm much resembles my brother who died," said Beautiful Sara. "All the angels are alike," answered the Rabbi spontaneously; and taking his wife by the hand he led her through the dense crowd on the shore, where, as it was the time of the Easter Fair, stood a great number of newly-erected wooden booths. Then passing through the dark Main River Gate into the city, they found themselves amid quite as noisy a multitude. Here in a narrow street one shop stood close by another, every house, as was usual in Frankfurt, being specially adapted to trade. There were no windows on the ground floor, but broad open arches, so that the passer-by, looking deep into the interior, could see at a glance all there was for sale. And how Beautiful Sara was astonished at the mass of magnificent wares, and the splendour, such as she had never seen before! Here stood Venetians, who offered for sale all the elegancies and luxuries of the East and Italy, and Beautiful Sara seemed as if enchanted by the ornaments and jewels, the coloured and varied caps and bodices, the gold bangles and necklaces, and the whole display of knick-knackery which women look at so lovingly and wear even more endearingly. The richly embroidered stuffs of velvet and silk seemed to speak to Beautiful Sara, and flash and sparkle back strange wonders into her memory, and it really seemed to her as if she were again a little girl, and that Aunt Birdy had kept her promise and taken her to the Frankfurt Fair, and that she now at last stood before the beautiful garments of which she had heard so much. With a secret joy she reflected what she should take back with her to Bacherach, and which of her two little cousins, Flowery and Birdy, would prefer that blue silk sash, and whether the green trousers would suit little Gottschalk—when all at once it flashed on her, "Ah, Lord! they are all grown up now, and yesterday they were slain!" She shuddered and shrank into herself, and the shadows of the night seemed to settle again in her soul; but the gold-embroidered cloths glittered once more with a thousand roguish eyes, and drove dark thoughts from her mind, and as she looked into her husband's face it was free from clouds, and bore its habitual serious gentleness. "Shut your eyes, Sara!" said the Rabbi, and led his wife still onward through the crowd.

What a varied, variegated, multitude! For the most part they were the tradesmen, who loudly outbid one another in offering bargains, or talked to themselves, summing on their fingers, or, followed by porters bearing high-packed loads, who at a dog-trot led the way to their lodgings. By the faces of others one could see that they came from curiosity. The portly councilman was recognizable by his scarlet cloak and golden chain, while the black, prosperous puffed waistcoat betrayed the honourable and proud patricians. The iron-peaked helmet, the yellow leather jerkin, and the rattling spurs, weighing one pound, indicated the heavy cavalryman, or squire. Under many a little black velvet cap, which bowed in a point over the brow, there hid a rosy girl-face, and the young fellows who jumped after it, like hunting-dogs on the scent, showed they were finished dandies by their saucily feathered caps, their rattling peaked shoes, and their silk garments of separate colours, where one side was green and the other red, or the right striped like a rainbow, and the left in harlequin squares of many colours, so that the mad youths looked as if they were split in two. Propelled by the crowd, the Rabbi with his wife reached the Römer. This is the great market-place of the city, surrounded by houses with high gables, and takes its name from one immense building, "the Römer," which was bought by the magistracy and dedicated as the court-house or town-hall. In it the German Emperor was elected, and tournaments were often held in front of it. King Max-imilian, who was passionately fond of such sports, was then in Frankfurt, and in his honour, the day before, there had been great tilting in the Römer ground. Many idle men still stood on or about the scaffolding, which was being dis-mantled by carpenters, and told how the Duke of Brunswick and the Margrave of Brandenburg had charged one another amid the sound of drums and of trumpets, and how Lord Walter the Blackguard had knocked the Knight of the Bear so soundly out of his saddle that the splinters of the lances flew high in the air, and the tall blonde King Max, standing upon the balcony among his courtiers, rub-bed his hands for joy. Covers of gold cloth were still to be seen on the balustrades and the balconies and in the Gothic windows of the town-hall. The other houses of the market-place were also still bedecked and adorned with shields, especially the Limburg house, on whose banner was painted a maiden who bore a sparrow-hawk on her hand, while a monkey held out to her a mirror. Many knights and ladies stood on the balcony engaged in merry conversation, while looking at the crowd below, which, in odd groups and as odd attire, shifted here and there. What a multitude of idlers and loiterers of all ages and stations crowded to-gether here to gratify curiosity! There was laughing, grum-bling, stealing, pinching, hurrahing, while ever and anon was heard in yelling, braying notes the trumpet of the mountebank quack, who, in a red cloak with his Jack Pudding and monkey, stood on a high stand blowing bra-vely the horn of his own skill, and sounding the praises of his tinctures and marvellous salves, ere he solemnly re-garded the glass of urine brought by some old woman, or applied himself to pull a poor peasant's back tooth. Two

fencing-masters, fluttering about in gay ribbons, brandishing their rapiers, met as if by chance, and had a mock duel, with great apparent anger; but after a long assault-at-arms each declared that the other was invincible, and took up a collection. Then the newly-organised guild of archers marched by with drummers and pipers, and these were followed by the prison guard, who carried a red flag, and led a bevy of travelling disreputable women, who came from the woman's house, known as "the Ass," in Würzburg, and were going to the Rosendale, where the highly honourable municipal authority had assigned them their quarters for the fair. "Shut your eyes, Sara," said the Rabbi. For indeed the fantastic crowd of very scantily-clad girls—some of them, really beautiful, behaved in a most unseemly manner, baring their bold white breasts, chaffing those who went by with shameless words, and swinging their long walking sticks. And as they came to the gate of Saint Katherine they rode on them as children on hobby horses, and sang in shrill tones the witch-song—

> "Where is the goat? the hellish beast;
> Where is the goat? Oh bring him quick!
> And if there is no goat, at least
> We'll ride upon the stick."

This wild sing-song, which rang afar, was lost in the long-drawn solemn tones of an approaching church procession. It was a mournful train of bare-headed and bare-footed monks, who carried burning wax tapers, banners with pictures of the saints, and great silver crucifixes. Before it ran boys clad in red and white gowns, bearing smoking censers of frankincense. In the midst, under a splendid canopy, were priests in white choir robes, bedecked with costly lace or in many-coloured stoles, and one of them held in his hand a sun-like golden vessel, which on arriving at a shrine by the market-corner he raised on high, while he half-sang, half-spoke in Latin—when all at once a little bell rang, and all around becoming silent, fell on their knees and made the sign of the Cross. "Shut your eyes, Sara!" said the Rabbi again, and hastily drew her away through a labyrinth of narrow and crooked side streets, and at last over the desolate empty place which separated the new Jewish quarter from the rest of the city.

Before that time the Jews dwelt between the Cathedral and the bank of the Main River that is, from the bridge to the Lumpenbrunnen and from the Mehlwage as far as Saint Bartholomew's. But the Catholic priests obtained a Papal bull forbidding the Jews to live so near the main church, for which reason the magistrates assigned them a place on the Wollgraben, where they built their present quarter. This was surrounded with strong walls, and had iron chains before the gate to shut them in from the press of a mob. Here they lived, crowded and fearful, and with far more vivid memories of previous suffering than at present. In 1240 the raging populace had caused an awful "bath of blood" among them, which was remembered as the first Jewish massacre; and in 1349, when the Flagellants, while passing through the town, set fire to it, and accused the Jews of the deed: the latter were nearly all murdered or burned alive in their own houses by an aroused mob. This was called the second Jewish massacre. After this the Jews were often threatened with similar slaughter, and during the internal dissensions of Frankfurt, especially during a dispute of the council with the guilds, the mob was often on the point of attacking the Jewish quarter. This place had two doors, which on Catholic festivals were closed from without and on Jewish festivals from within, and before each gate was a guard-house with city soldiers.

As the Rabbi came with his wife to the entrance to the Jewish quarter, the soldiers lay, as one could see through the open windows, on the wooden bench of their guard-room, while outside, before the door, sat the drummer playing small caprices on his great drum. He was a power-fully built, heavy fellow, wearing a jerkin and hose of fiery yellow, greatly puffed out on the arms and thighs, and profusely scattered with small red sewed on tufts, which looked as if innumerable tongues were licking him from head to foot. His breast and back were covered with cushions of black cloth, against which hung his drum; he bore on his head a flat, round black cap, which was matched by his face in roundness and flatness, and which was in keeping with his dress, being also orange-yellow, picked out with black pimples, and contracted into a gap-ing smile. So the fellow sat and drummed the air of a song which the Flagellants had sung at the Jewish massacre, while he sang, in a rough, beery voice, gurgling the text:

> "Our dear Lady true
> Walked in the morning dew,
>   Kyrie eleison!"

"Hans, that is a terrible tune," cried a voice from behind the closed gate of the Jewish quarter. "Yes, Hans, and a bad song too—don't suit the drum; don't suit at all—by my soul—not the fair and not the Easter morning—bad song—dangerous song, Hans, Hansie! Little Hansie, the drum-mer—I'm a lonely man—and if you love me, the Stern, the tall Stern, the tall Schnozzle Stern, then stop it!"

These words were forced out in fragments by the unseen speaker, now as in hasty anxiety, anon in a sighing drawl, with a tone which alternated from drawn-out softness to harsh hoarseness, such as one hears in consumptive peo-ple. The drummer was not moved, and continued his song—

"There came a little youth,
His first beard showed, in truth,
                                   Halleluja!

"Hans," again cried the voice of the above mentioned invisible speaker, "Hans, I'm a lone man, and it is a dangerous song, and I don't like hearing it; and I have my reasons for it, and if you love me sing something else, and to-morrow we will drink together."

At the word "drink" Hans ceased his drumming and singing, and said in a regular tone, "The devil take the Jews! but you, dear Schnozzle Stern, are my friend, I protect you; and if we should only drink together often enough I will even convert you. Yea, I will be your god-father, and when baptized you will be eternally happy; and if you have genius and will study industriously under me you may even become a drummer. Yes, schnozzle Stern, you may yet become something great. I will drum the whole catechism into you when we drink tomorrow together; but now open the gate, for here are two strangers who wish to enter."

"Open the gate?" shrieked Schnozzle Stern, and his voice almost deserted him. "That can't be done in such a hurry, my dear Hans; one can't tell—just can't tell—and I'm a lone man. Veitel Rindskopf has the key, and he is now standing still in the corner mumbling his Prayer of Eighteen Benedictions, which must not be interrupted. And Jäkel the Fool is here too, but he is busy; I'm a lone man."

"The devil take the Jews!" cried the drummer, and laughing loudly at his own joke, he trundled himself to the guard-room and also lay down on the bench.

While the Rabbi waited with his wife alone before the great locked gate, there rose from behind it a strangely ringing, nasal, and somewhat mocking slow voice. "little Stern, don't drone and groan so long. Take the keys from

Rindskopf's coat pockets, or else go stick your nose in the keyhole, and unlock the gate with it. The people have been standing and waiting a long time."

"People!" cried the voice of the fellow known as Schnozzle Stern, as if frightened. "I thought there was only one; and I beg you, Fool—dear Jäkel Fool—look out and see who are there."

A small, well-grated window in the gate opened, and there appeared in it a yellow cap with two horns, and the drolly, wrinkled, and twisted jest-maker's face of Jäkel the Fool. At once the peephole window was shut, and he cried angrily, "Open the gate—there is only a man and a woman."

"A man and a wo-man!" groaned Schnozzle Stern. "Yes, and when the gate's opened the woman will take her gown off, and is also a man; and there'll be two men, and we are only three!"

"Don't be a scaredy-hare," replied Jäkel the Fool. "Pick up your heart and show courage!"

"Courage!" cried Schnozzle Stern and laughed with mournful bitterness. "Scaredy Hare! Hare is a bad comparison. The hare is an unclean beast. Courage! I am not put here to be courageous, but cautious. When too many come I am supposed to scream. But I alone cannot keep them back. My arm is weak, I have an issue-sore, and I'm a lone man. If they shoot at me I shall die. Then that rich man, Mendel Reiss, will sit on the Sabbath at his table, and wipe the raisin sauce from his mouth, and rub his belly, and perhaps say, "Tall Schnozzle Stern was a brave little fellow after all; if it had not been for him perhaps they would have burst the gate. He let himself be shot dead for us. He was a brave little fellow; pity that he's dead!"

Here the voice became gradually tender and tearful, but all at once it rose to a hasty and almost angry tone. "Courage! and because the rich Mendel Reiss wipes away the raisin sauce from his mouth, and pats his belly, and calls me a brave little fellow, I'm to let myself be shot dead! Courage! Be brave! Little Strauss was brave, and yesterday went to the Römer to see the tilting, and thought they would not know him because he wore a frock of violet velvet—three florins a yard—with fox-tails all embroidered with gold—quite magnificent; and they dusted his violet frock for him till it lost its colour, and his own back became violet and did not look human. Courage, indeed! The crooked, crippled Leser was courageous, and called our black-guardly chief magistrate a blackguard, and they hung him up by the feet between two dogs while Jack drummed. Courage! Don't be a hare! Among many dogs the hare is lost. I'm a lone man, and I am really afraid."

"That I'll swear to," cried Jäkel.

"Yes; I *have* fear," replied Schnozzle Stern, sighing. "I know that fear runs in my blood, and I had it from my late mother"—

"Ay, ay," interrupted Jäkel, "and your mother had it from her father, and he from his, and so all ancestors one from the other, back to the forefather who marched with King Saul against the Philistines, and was the first to run away. But look! Rindskopf is all ready—he has bowed his head for the fourth time; now he is jumping like a flea at the Holy, Holy, Holy, and seeking cautiously in his pocket."

In fact the keys rattled, the gate grated and creaked as it opened, and the Rabbi and his wife entered the empty Judengasse. The man who opened was a little fellow with a good-natured sour face, who nodded absently, like one who did not like to be disturbed in his thoughts, and when he had carefully once more closed the portal, slipped without saying a word into a corner behind the gate, still murmuring his prayers. Less taciturn was Jäkel the Fool, a short fellow with bandy legs, a full blooming, red, and laughing face, and an enormous leg-of-mutton hand, which he stretched out of the wide sleeve of his chequered jacket in welcome. Behind him a tall, lean figure showed or rather hid itself—the slender neck white feathered with a fine cambric ruff, and the thin pale face strangely adorned with an incredibly long nose, which anxiously peered about in every direction.

"God's welcome to a pleasant feast-day!" cried Jäkel the Fool. "Do not be astonished that the lane is so empty and silent just now. All our people are in the synagogue, and you are come just in the right time to hear the history of the sacrifice of Isaac being read. I know it—'tis an interesting tale, and if I had not heard it before, thirty-three times, I would willingly hear it again this year. And—mind you!— 'tis an important history, for if Abraham had really slaughtered Isaac and not the ram, then there would have been more rams in the world now—and fewer Jews." And then, with madly merry grimaces, Jäkel began to sing the following song from the *Agade*:

"A kid, a kid, which my father bought for two pieces of money. A kid! A kid!

"There came a cat which ate the kid, which my father bought for two pieces of money. A kid!

"There came a dog, who bit the cat, who ate the kid, which my father bought for two pieces of money. A kid!

"There came a stick, which beat the dog, who bit the cat, who ate the kid, which my father bought for two pieces of money. A kid! A kid!

"There came a fire, which burnt the stick, which beat the dog, who bit the cat, who ate the kid, which my father bought for two pieces of money. A kid! A kid!

"There came the water, which quenched the fire, which burnt the stick, which beat the dog, who bit the cat, who ate the kid, which my father bought for two pieces of money. A kid! A kid!

"There came an ox, who drank the water, which

quenched the fire, which burnt the stick, which beat the dog, who bit the cat, who ate the kid, which my father bought for two pieces of money. A kid! A kid!

"There came the butcher, who slew the ox, who drank the water, which quenched the fire, which burnt the stick, which beat the dog, who bit the cat, that ate the kid, which my father bought for two pieces of money. A kid! A kid!

"Then came the Angel of Death, who slew the butcher, who killed the ox, who drank the water, which quenched the fire, which burnt the stick, which beat the dog, who bit the cat, who ate the kid, which my father bought for two pieces of money. A kid! kid!"

"Yes, beautiful lady," added the singer, "and the day will come when the Angel of Death will slay the slayer, and all our blood come over Edom, for God is a God of vengeance."

But all at once, decidedly casting aside the seriousness into which he had unintentionally fallen, Jäkel jumped again into his mad fancies, and kept on in his grating jester tones, "Don't be afraid, beautiful lady, Schnozzle Stern will not harm you. He is only dangerous to the old Ellen Schnapper. She has fallen in love with his nose—and, faith! it deserves it. Yea, for it is beautiful as the tower which looketh forth towards Damascus, and lofty like a cedar of Lebanon. Outwardly it gleameth like gold leaf and syrup, and inwardly it is all music and loveliness. It bloometh in summer and in winter it is frozen up—but in summer and winter it is petted by the white hands of Ellen Schnapper. Yes, she is madly in love with him. She cuddles him, she fuddles and fodders him. When he is fat enough she means to marry him. For her age he is young enough. And whoever comes to Frankfurt, three hundred years hence, will not be able to see the heavens for Schnozzle Stern."

"Ah, you are Jäkel the Fool," exclaimed the Rabbi,

laughing. "I mark it by your words. I have often heard of you."

"Yes—yes," replied Jäkel, with a comical air of modesty. "Yes, that comes of being famous. A man is often celebrated far and wide for being a bigger fool than he has any idea of. However, I take great pains to do my very best to be a fool, and jump and shake myself to make the bells ring. Other people lead an easier life. But tell me, Rabbi, why do you journey on a festival day?"

"My justification," replied the Rabbi, "is in the Talmud, and it says, 'Danger drives away the Sabbath.'"

"Danger!" screamed the tall Schnozzle Stern, with an air of deadly terror. "Danger! danger! Hans the drummer!—drum, drum. Danger! danger! Hans the drummer!"

From without resounded the deep beery voice of Hans the drummer. "Damn it! The devil take the Jews. That's the third time today that you've woke me out of a sound sleep, Schnozzle Stern! Don't make me mad! For when I am mad I'm the howling old devil himself; and then as sure as I'm a Christian I'll up with my gun and shoot slap through the grated peephole of your tower—and then it'll be, old fellow, everybody look out for his nose!"

"Don't shoot! don't shoot! I'm a lonely man," wailed Schnozzle Stern piteously, and pressed his face against the nearest wall, and remained trembling and murmuring prayers in this position.

"But say, what has happened?" now cried Jäkel the Fool, with all the impatient curiosity which was even then characteristic of the Frankfurt Jews.

But the Rabbi impatiently broke loose from him and went his way along the Judengasse. "See, Sara!" he sighed, "how badly guarded is Israel. False friends guard its gates without, and within, its guardians are folly and fear."

The two wandered slowly through the long and empty street, where only here and there the head of a rosy young

girl looked out of a window, while the sun mirrored itself in the sparkling panes. In those days the houses in the Jewish quarter were still neat and new, and much lower than they now are, since it was only at a later time that the Jews, as their number greatly increased, although they were not permitted to enlarge their quarter, built one storey over another, squeezed themselves together like sardines, and so became crippled in both body and soul. That part of the Jewish quarter which remained after the great fire, and which is called the Old Lane—that series of high, dark houses, where strangely grimacing people bargain and chaffer all over the place, is a gruesome relic of the Middle Ages. The older synagogue exists no more; it was less capracious than the present one, built later, after the refugees from Nuremberg were taken into the community. It lay more to the north. The Rabbi had no need to ask his way. He found it from afar by the buzz of many voices often raised aloud. In the court of the House of God he parted from his wife, and after washing his hands at the fountain there, entered the lower part of the synagogue where the men pray, while Beautiful Sara went up a flight of stairs and came into the place reserved for women.

This upper portion was a kind of gallery with three rows of wooden seats painted of a reddish brown, whose backs were fitted with a hinged hanging board very convenient for holding the prayer-books. Here the women sat next to each other gossiping or standing up deep in prayer. However, they sometimes went and peered with curiosity through the large grating which was on the eastern side, through the thin green lattice of which one could look down into the lower portion of the synagogue. There, behind high praying-desks, stood the men in their black cloaks, their pointed beards jutting out over white ruffs, and their skull-capped heads more or less concealed by a four-cornered scarf of white wool or silk, furnished with the prescribed tassels, in some instances also adorned with gold lace. The walls of the synagogue were uniformly white-washed, and no other ornament was to be seen except the gilded iron grating around the square stage, where the portions from the Law were read, and the holy ark, a costly embossed chest, apparently upheld by marble columns with rich capitols, whose flower and leaf-work flourished charmingly, covered with a curtain of cornflower-blue velvet, on which a pious inscription was worked in gold spangles, pearls, and many-coloured gems. Here hung the silver memorial-lamp, and there also rose a barred dais, on whose crossed iron bars were all kinds of sacred utensils, among the rest the seven-branched candlestick; while before it, his countenance towards the ark, stood the cantor, whose song was accompanied as if instrumentally by the voices of his two assistants, the bass and the discant. For the Jews have forbidden all instrumental music, as such, to be used in their Church, thinking that hymns to God are more edifying when they rise from the glowing breast of man, than from the cold pipes of an organ. Beautiful Sara was pleased like a child when the cantor, an admirable tenor, raised his voice, and the ancient, solemn melodies which she knew so well bloomed forth in a fresher loveliness than she had ever dreamed of, while the bass intoned, contrasting, the deep dark notes, and in the intervals the discant trilled sweetly and daintily. Such singing Beautiful Sara had never heard in the synagogue of Bacherach, because the chairman of the congregation, David Levi, acted as cantor; and when this trembling elderly man, with his broken baa-ing voice, would try to trill like a girl, and in his desperate effort to do so shook his weak and drooping arm feverishly, the sight inspired laughter rather than devotion.

A something of devotion; not unmingled with feminine curiosity, drew Beautiful Sara to the grating, where she could look down into the lower section, or the so-called

men's school. She had never before seen so many of her faith together, and it cheered her heart profoundly to be in such a multitude of those so nearly allied by background, thought, and suffering. And her soul was still more deeply moved when three old men reverentially approached the holy ark, pushed the shiny curtain aside, opened the ark, and very carefully took out that Book which God once wrote with His own hand, and to maintain which the Jews have suffered so much—so much misery and hate, disgrace and death—a thousand years' martyrdom. This Book—a great roll of parchment—was wrapped like a princely child in a gaily embroidered scarlet velvet mantle; above, on both the wooden rollers, were two little silver shrines, in which many pomegranates and small bells moved and rang prettily, while before, on a silver chain, hung gold shields with coloured gems. The cantor took the Book and, as if it had been really a child—a child for whom one has greatly suffered and whom one loves all the more on that account— he rocked it in his arms, lightly danced with it hither and thither, pressed it to his breast and, like one thrilled by that touch, broke forth into such a jubilantly devout hymn of praise and thanksgiving that Beautiful Sara fancied she saw the pillars of the holy shrine begin to bloom, the strange and lovely blossoms and leaves of the capitols grow taller and taller, and the notes of the treble change to nightingales, while the vault of the synagogue was cleft by the mighty tones of the bass singer, the joy of God beaming down from the blue heavens. Yes, it was a beautiful psalm. The congregation repeated the concluding verse in chorus, and the cantor walked slowly to the raised platform in the middle of the synagogue, carrying the holy Book, while men and boys crowded about him to kiss, or only to touch, its velvet covering. On the described platform, the velvet mantle was removed from the holy Book and the binders, covered with illuminated letters, were unwound, and the cantor, in the singing intonation which in the Passover service is still more special, read the edifying story of the trial of Abraham.

The Beautiful Sara had modestly stepped back from the grating, and a stout, overly decorated woman of middle age, looking self-assured and good-natured, had, with a nod, let her share her prayerbook. This lady was evidently no great scholar, for as she murmured the prayers to herself as the women do, not being allowed to take part in the singing, Sara noted that she made the best she could of many words and slurred over not a few good lines altogether. But after a while, the good woman languidly raised her water-clear eyes, and a noncommittal smile passed over her face which was red and white like porcelain. In a voice which she strove to make as genteel as possible, she said to the Beautiful Sara: "He sings very well. But I have heard far better singing in Holland. You are a stranger, and perhaps do not know that the cantor is from Worms, and that they will keep him here if he will be content with four hundred florins a year. He is a charming man, and his hands are as white as alabaster. I think a great deal of a handsome hand; it makes one altogether handsome"—saying which, the good lady, with some self-satisfaction, laid her own still beautiful hand on the shelf before her, and with a polite bow which intimated that she did not care to be interrupted while speaking, she added, "The little singer is a mere child, and looks very emaciated. The basso is too ugly for anything, and our Stern once said—it was very witty of him—'The bass singer is a bigger fool than a basso is expected to be!' All three take their meals in my eating place—perhaps you don't know that I'm Ellen Schnapper?"

Beautiful Sara expressed her thanks for the information, when Ellen Schnapper proceeded to narrate in detail how she had once been in Amsterdam, how she had been subjected to base designs on account of her remarkable beauty, how she had come to Frankfurt three days before Pentecost and married Schnapper, how he had passed away, and what touching things he had said on his deathbed, and how hard it was to carry on the business of an eating-shop and keep one's hands nice. Several times she glanced aside with contemptuous looks, apparently directed at some sneering young women who were apparently sizing up her clothes. Truly this dress was remarkable enough—a very puffed skirt of white satin, on which all the animals of Noah's Ark were embroidered in gaudy colours; a jacket of cloth of gold like a cuirass, the sleeves of red velvet slashed with yellow; on her head, a superhumanly tall cap; round her neck, a mighty ruff of stiff white linen; furthermore a silver chain, hung with all kinds of coins, cameos, and curiosities, chief among which was a great image of the city of Amsterdam, which rested on her bosom.

But the dresses of the other women were not less remarkable. They consisted of a medley of fashions of different ages, and many a little woman there was so covered with gold and diamonds as to look like a walking jeweller's shop. A certain kind of garb was, indeed, imposed by law upon the Jews of Frankfurt in those days. To distinguish them from Christians, the men had to wear yellow rings on their cloaks, and the women very high standing, blue striped veils on their caps. However, within the Jewish quarter, these laws were scarcely heeded, and there, especially on festivals and even more in the synagogue, the women competed in coming up with as much finery as they could— partly to arouse envy in the others, and partly to advertise the wealth and credit rating of their husbands.

While downstairs in the synagogue, passages from the Books of Moses are being read, the devotion is apt to relax somewhat. Many make themselves comfortable and sit down, whispering with a friend about mundane affairs, or one might go out into the courtyard to get a little fresh air. Small boys take the liberty of visiting their mothers in the women's gallery where the worshipful mood has suffered an even greater decline. There's chatting, gossiping, laughing, and, as will always happen, the younger women make fun of the elder, while the latter complain of youth and the general degeneracy of the times. And just as there was a cantor downstairs in the synagogue of Frankfurt, so there was a headcackler and gossip in the second floor, above. This was Puppy Reiss, a flat, greenish woman who had a nose for every bit of trouble and always some scandal on her tongue. The usual target of her pointed remarks was the poor Ellen Schnapper, and she could imitate very drolly the affected gentility and languishing manner with which the latter accepted the mock-compliments of young men. "Do you know" Puppy Reiss cried now, "that Ellen Schnapper said yesterday, 'If I were not beautiful and clever, and beloved, I had rather not live.' "

There was some loud tittering, and Ellen Schnapper who stood near, noted that this was all at her expense. She raised her eyes disdainfully and sailed away like a proud and majestic ship to a more distant place. Then Birdie Ochs, a plump and somewhat awkward lady, remarked compassionately that Ellen Schnapper might be a little vain and small of mind, but that she was a kind and generous soul, and did much good to many folk in need.

"Particularly to Schnozzle Stern," snapped Puppy Reiss. And all who knew of this tender tie laughed all the louder.

"Don't you know," added Puppy spitefully, "that Schnozzle Stern now sleeps in Ellen Schnapper's house! But just look at Susy Flörsheim down there, wearing the necklace which Daniel Fläsch pawned to her husband! Fläsch's wife is vexed at it—*that* is plain. And now she is talking to Mrs. Flörsheim. *How* amiably they shake hands!—and hate one another like Midian and Moab! How sweetly they smile on one another! Oh, you dear souls, *don't* eat one another up out of pure tenderness! I'll just steal up and listen to them!"

And so, like a sneaking wild cat, Puppy Reiss stole along and heard the two women mutually bewailing to one another how they had worked themselves to the bone all the past week to clean up the house and scour the cooking utensils, and all they had to do before Passover, so that not a crumb of leavened bread stuck to anything. And such troubles as they had baking the unleavened bread! Mrs. Fläsch had bitter grievances over this—for she had no end of trouble over it in the community bakery, for according to the ticket which she drew she could not bake there until the last days, on the very eve of the festival, and late in the afternoon, too!—; and then old Hannah had kneaded the dough badly, and the maids had rolled it too thin, and half of it was scorched in baking, and worst of all, rain dripped constantly through the slats on the bake-house roof, and so, wet and weary, they had to work far into the night.

"And, my dear Mrs. Flörsheim," said Mrs. Fläsch, with considerate friendliness which did not sound sincere, "you were a little to blame for that, because you did not send your people to help me in baking."

"Ah! pardon," replied the other. "My help was just too occupied—the goods for the fair had to be packed—we are so terribly busy at this time—my husband"—

"Yes. I know," interrupted Mrs. Fläsch, with cutting haste and irony. "I know that you have much to do—many pledges and a good business, and necklaces"—

And a bitter word was just about to glide from the lips of the speaker, and Dame Flörsheim had turned as red as a lobster, when Puppy Reiss screeched loudly, "For God's sake!—the strange lady lies dying—water! water!"

Beautiful Sara lay insensible, pale as death, while a swarm of women, busy and bewailing, crowded round her. One held her head, another her arm, some old women sprinkled her with the small glasses of water which hung behind their prayer desks for washing the hands in case they should by accident touch their own bodies. Others held under her nose an old lemon stuck full of cloves, which remained from the last fast-day, when it had served for smelling and strengthening the nerves. Exhausted and sighing deeply, Beautiful Sara at last opened her eyes, and with mute glances thanked them for their kind care. But now the Prayer of Eighteen Benedictions which no one dare neglect, was beginning to be solemnly intoned below, and the busy women hurried back to their places and offered the prayer as the rite ordains, standing up, with their faces turned towards the east, which is the direction in which Jerusalem lies. Birdie Ochs, Ellen Schnapper, and Puppy Reiss stayed longest by Beautiful Sara—the first two eagerly offering to aid her, the latter to find out once more why it was that she fainted so suddenly.

But Beautiful Sara had swooned from a singular cause. It is a custom in the synagogue that any one who has escaped a great danger shall, after the reading of the extracts from the Law, step forward and return thanks to the Divine Providence for his deliverance. As Rabbi Abraham rose in the multitude to recite this prayer, and Beautiful Sara recognised her husband's voice, she observed how its tone gradually passed into the mournful murmur of the prayer for the dead. She heard the names of her dear ones and relations, accompanied, moreover, by the benedictory epithet appropriate to the departed; and the last hope vanished from her soul, for it was torn by the certainty that those dear ones had really been slain, that her little niece was dead, that her little cousins, Flory and Birdy, were dead, that little Gottschalk was dead too. All murdered and dead. And she too would have died from the agony of this conviction, had not a beneficent swoon poured forgetfulness over her senses.

THIRD CHAPTER

When Beautiful Sara, after divine service was ended, went down into the courtyard of the synagogue, the Rabbi stood there waiting for her. He nodded to her with a cheerful expression, and accompanied her out into the street, where there was no longer silence but a noisy multitude. It was like a stream of ants, what with bearded men in black coats, women gleaming along like gold-chafers, boys in new clothes carrying prayer-books after their parents, young girls who, because they could not enter the synagogue, now came bounding out of their houses to meet their parents, bowing their curly heads to receive their blessings—all serene and merry, and walking up and down the street with the happy anticipations of people expecting a good midday meal, the exquisite scent of which caused the mouth to water. It rose from many black pots which were identified with chalk and were being fetched by smiling girls from the great community kitchen.

In this multitude there was specially notable a Spanish cavalier, whose youthful features bore that fascinating pallor which ladies generally associate with an unfortunate—and men, on the contrary, with a very fortunate—love affair. His gait, sauntering, had however in it a somewhat affected daintiness; the feathers of his cap were more agitated by the aristocratic waving of his head than by the wind; and his golden spurs, and the trappings of his sword, which he bore on his arm, rattled rather more than was needed. A costly sword hilt could be seen gleaming under a white cavalier's cloak which enveloped his slender limbs in an apparently careless manner, which, however, betrayed the most careful arrangement of the folds. Passing and repassing, partly with curiosity, partly with an air of a connoisseur, he approached the women walking by, looked calmly and steadily at them, paused when he thought a face

was worth the trouble, gave to many a pretty girl a passing
compliment, and went his way heedless as to its effect. He
had circled Beautiful Sara more than once, but seemed to
be repelled every time by her commanding look, or the
enigmatically smiling air of her husband, but at last,
proudly subduing all diffidence, he boldly faced both, and
with foppish confidence delivered the following address in a
tenderly gallant tone:

"I swear, Senora!—listen to me!—I swear—by the roses
of both the kingdoms of Castile, by the Aragonese hya-
cinths and the pomegranate blossoms of Andalusia! by the
sun which illumines all Spain, with all its flowers, onions,
pea-soups, forests, mountains, mules, he-goats, and Old
Christians! by the canopy of heaven, of which this sun is
only the golden tassel! and by the God who sits on the roof
of heaven and meditates day and night over the creation of
new forms of lovely women!—I swear that you, Senora, are
the fairest dame whom I have seen in all the German realm,
and if you please to accept my service, then I pray of you
the favour, grace, and leave to call myself your knight and
bear your colours henceforth in jest or earnest!"

A flush as of pain rose in the face of Beautiful Sara, and
with one of those glances which are the most cutting from
the gentlest eyes, and with a tone which sounds most devas-
tating from a soft voice, the lady answered, deeply hurt:—

"My noble lord, if you will be my knight you must fight
whole races, and such a battle wins little thanks and even
less honour; and if you want to wear my colours, then you
must sew yellow rings on your cloak, or bind you with a
blue-striped scarf, for such are my colours—the colours of
my house, the House called Israel, which is wretched in-
deed, one mocked in the streets by the sons of good for-
tune."

A sudden purple red shot into the cheeks of the Span-
iard; deepest confusion showed in all his features and he

stammered as he said:

"Senora, you misunderstood me. An innocent jest—but, by God, no mockery, no jest at Israel. I myself am sprung from the House of Israel . . . my grandfather was a Jew, perhaps even my father."

"And it is very certain, Senor, that your uncle is one," suddenly joined in the Rabbi, who had calmly witnessed this scene; and with a merry quizzical glance he added, "And I myself will be bound that Don Isaac Abarbanel, nephew of the great Rabbi, is sprung from the best blood of Israel, if not from the royal line of David!"

The chain of the sword rattled under the Spaniard's cloak, his cheeks became deadly white again, his upper lip twitched as with scorn as it battles pain, and angry death grinned in his eyes as in an utterly changed, ice-cold, keen staccato voice he said:—

"Senor Rabbi, you know me. Well, then, you know also who I am. And if the fox knows that I belong to the breed of the lion, let him beware and not bring his fox-beard into danger of death, nor provoke my anger. How can the fox judge the lion? Only he who feels like the lion can understand his weaknesses."

"Oh, I understand well," answered the Rabbi, and a sad seriousness came over his brow. "I understand well, how the proud lion, out of pride, casts aside his princely hide and goes mumming in the scaly armour of a crocodile, because it is the fashion to be a grinning, cunning, greedy crocodile! What can you expect the lesser beasts to be when the lion denies his nature? But beware, Don Isaac, you were not made for the crocodile's element. For water—you know well what I mean—is your evil fortune, and you will perish. Water is not your element; the weakest trout can live in it better than the king of the forest. Have you forgotten how the current of the Tagus almost swallowed you?"

Bursting into loud laughter, Don Isaac suddenly threw

his arms round the Rabbi's neck, covered his mouth with kisses, leapt for joy high into the air, his spurs jingling, so that the Jews who were passing by shrank back and in his own naturally cordial and joyous voice he cried—

"Truly you are Abraham of Bacherach! And it was a good joke, and more than that, an act of friendship, when you—in Toledo—leapt from the Alcantara bridge into the water, and grasped by the hair your friend, who could drink better than he could swim, and drew him to dry land. I was very near making really deep research whether there are actually grains of gold at the bottom of the Tagus, and whether the Romans were right in calling it the golden river. I assure you that I catch cold even now from only thinking of that water-party."

Saying this the Spaniard made a gesture as if he were shaking drops of water from his garments. The countenance of the Rabbi expressed great joy and he again and again pressed his friend's hand, saying every time—

"I am indeed glad."

"And so indeed am I," answered the other. "It is seven years now since we last saw each other, and when we parted I was only a little greenhorn, and you—you were already so staid and serious. But whatever became of the beautiful Donna who in those days cost you so many sighs, rhyming sighs, which you accompanied with the lute?"

"Hush, hush! the Donna hears us—she is my wife, and you have yourself presented her to-day with a sample of your taste and poetic skill."

It was not without some trace of his former embarrassment that the Spaniard greeted the beautiful lady, who amiably regretted that she had pained a friend of her husband by her expression of displeasure.

"Ah, Senora," replied Don Isaac, "he who stretches out his clumsy hand towards a rose must not complain that the thorns scratch. When the star of evening mirrors itself, gold-gleaming, in the azure stream—

"For God's sake! Stop that!" interrupted the Rabbi, "If we wait till the star of evening mirrors itself, gold-gleaming in the azure stream, my wife will starve, for she has eaten nothing since yesterday, and suffered much misfortune and discomfort in the meantime."

"Well, then, I will take you to Israel's best eating place," said Don Isaac, "to the house of my friend Ellen Schnapper, which is not far away. I already smell the sweet perfume of the kitchen! Oh, if you only knew, O Abraham, how this perfume woos and wins me. This it is which, since I have dwelt in this city, so often lures me to the tents of Jacob. Intimacy with God's peculiar people is not a weakness of mine, and truly it is not to pray but to eat that I visit the Jews' Street."

"You have never loved us, Don Isaac."

"Well," continued the Spaniard, "I like your cooking much better than your faith which lacks the right sauce. As for you, I really never could rightly digest you. Even in your best days, under the rule of my ancestor David, who was king over Judah and Israel, I never could have put up with you and would certainly, one fine morning, have run away from Mount Zion and emigrated to Phoenicia or Babylon where the joys of life sparkled in the temple of the gods."

"You blaspheme the one God, Isaac," murmured the Rabbi grimly. "You are much worse than a Christian—you are a heathen, an idolator."

"Yes, I am a heathen, and the melancholy selftormenting Nazarenes are quite as little to my taste as the dry and joyless Hebrews. May our dear Lady of Sidon, holy Astarte, forgive me, that I kneel to pray before the sorrowful Mother of the Crucified. Only my knee and my tongue worship death—my heart remained faithful to life."

"But do not look so sour," continued the Spaniard as he

saw how little his speech seemed to have pleased the Rabbi. "Do not look at me with abhorrence. My nose is not a renegade. When once, by chance, I came at dinner time into this street, and the well known savoury odour of the Jewish kitchen rose to my nose, I was seized by the same yearning which our fathers felt when they remembered the fleshpots of Egypt—pleasant tasting memories of youth came to me. I saw again in my mind the carp with brown raisin sauce which my aunt knew how to prepare so edifyingly for Friday evening. I saw once more the steamed mutton with garlic and horse-radish, fit to raise the dead, and the soup with dreamily swimming dumplings—and my soul melted like the notes of an enamoured nightingale— and since then I eat in the shop of my friend Donna Ellen Schnapper."

Meanwhile they had arrived at the place so highly praised, where Ellen Schnapper herself stood at the door greeting in a friendly manner the strangers come to the fair, who hungrily pushed their way in. Behind her and craning his head over her shoulder, was the tall Schnozzle Stern, anxiously and inquisitively examining all comers. Don Isaac approached the hostess with exaggerated grand style, who returned his satirically deep reverences with endless curtseys, after which he drew the glove from his right hand, wound it about with the fold of his cloak, and grasping that of Ellen Schnapper, drew it over his moustaches and said:—

"Senora! your eyes rival the glow of the sun! But unlike eggs the longer they are boiled the harder they become, my heart, on the contrary grows softer the longer it is cooked in the flaming rays of your eyes. From the yolk of my heart flies up the winged god Amor and seeks a confiding nest in your bosom. And oh, Senora, wherewith shall I compare that bosom? For in all the world there is no flower, no fruit, which is like to it! It is unique! Though the storm wind

tears away the leaves from the tenderest rose, your bosom is still a winter rose which defies all storms. Though the sour lemon the older it grows becomes yellower and more wrinkled, your bosom rivals in colour and softness the sweetest pineapple. Oh, Senora, if the city of Amsterdam be as beautiful as you told me yesterday, and the day before, and every day, yet is the ground on which it rests far lovelier still."

The cavalier spoke these last words with affected timidity, and ogled as if yearning at the great picture which hung from Ellen Schnapper's neck. Schnozzle Stern looked down with inquisitive eyes, and the much praised bosom heaved so billowy that the city of Amsterdam wobbled from side to side.

"Ah!" sighed Ellen Schnapper, "virtue is more precious than beauty. What use is my beauty to me? My youth is passing away, and since Schnapper is gone—at least, he had handsome hands—what use is beauty to me?"

With that she sighed again, and like an echo all but inaudible Schnozzle Stern sighed behind her.

"Of what avail is your beauty?" cried Don Isaac. "Oh, Donna Ellen Schnapper, do not sin against the goodness of creative Nature! Do not scorn her most gracious gifts. She will terribly revenge herself. Those beatific eyes will be like dim glasses, those winsome lips grow flat and commonplace, that chaste and charming form be changed into a barrel of tallow hardly pleasing to any one, and the city of Amsterdam at last rest on a musty bog."

So he sketched piece by piece the appearance of Ellen Schnapper, so that the poor woman was bewildered, and sought to escape the uncanny compliments of the cavalier. She was doubly delighted at this instant to see Beautiful Sara appear, as it gave her an opportunity to inquire whether she had quite recovered from her swoon. And so she rushed into lively chatter, in which she fully developed

79

her sham gentility mingled with real kindness of heart, and related with more breadth than depth the awful story how she herself had almost fainted with horror when she, innocent and inexperienced, came in a canal boat to Amsterdam, and the rascally porter who carried her trunk led her—not to a respectable tavern, but oh, horrors!—to an infamous place! She saw what it was the moment she entered, by the brandy-drinking; and, oh!—the improper suggestions!—and she would, as she said, "really have swooned, if it had not been that during the six weeks she stayed there she only once ventured to close her eyes."

"I dared not," she added, "on account of my virtue. And all that happened to me because of my beauty! But virtue will stay—when good looks pass away."

Don Isaac was beginning to go somewhat critically into the details of this story when, fortunately, Squinting Aaron Hirschkuh from Homburg on the Lahn came out of the house, a white apron in his mouth, and bitterly bewailed that the soup was already served, and that the guests were seated at table, but that the hostess was missing.

(The conclusion and the chapters which follow are lost, not from any fault of the author.)

Shylock (Jessica)

BY HEINRICH HEINE

Translated into English by Frederic Ewen

The Ghetto in Venice

When I saw this play presented in Drury Lane, there stood back of me in the box a pale British beauty who wept violently at the end of the fourth act and frequently cried out, "The poor man is wronged!" Hers was a face of the noblest Grecian cut, and her eyes were large and black. I could never forget them, those great black eyes, that wept for Shylock.

But when I think of those tears, I am forced to include *The Merchant of Venice* among the tragedies, although its frame is embellished with the gayest masks, pictures of satyrs and cupids, and the poet actually intended this to be a comedy. Perhaps Shakespeare wished to present an unmitigated werewolf for the amusement of the crowd, an abhorrent mythical creature that thirsts for blood, in the end loses his daughter and his ducats, and is made ridiculous into the bargain. But the poet's genius, the universal spirit which reigned in him, was always stronger than his own will, and so it happened that despite the exaggerated burlesque, he embodies in Shylock a justification of the hapless sect which for mysterious reasons had been burdened by Providence with the hatred on the part of the lower and higher rabble, and would not always requite this hatred with love.

But what am I saying? The genius of Shakespeare rises above the petty quarrels of two religious sects, and his drama in reality exhibits neither Jews nor Christians, but oppressors and oppressed, and the madly agonized jubilation of the latter when they can repay their arrogant tormentors with interest for insults inflicted on them.

There is not a trace of religious differences in this play. In Shylock Shakespeare shows us nothing but a man bidden by nature to hate his enemies—just as in Antonio and his friends he surely does not depict disciples of that divine doctrine which commands us to love our enemies. When Shylock says to the man who would borrow money from him:

> "Signor Antonio, many a time and oft
> In the Rialto, you have rated me
> About my monies and my usances:
> Still have I borne it with a patient shrug,
> For sufferance is the badge of all our tribe.
> You call me misbeliever, cut-throat dog,
> And spit upon my Jewish gaberdine,
> And all for use of that which is mine own.
> Well, then, it now appears you need my help:
> Go to then; you come to me, and you say,
> 'Shylock, we would have moneys:'—you say so;
> You, that did void your rheum upon my beard,
> And foot me as you spurn a stranger cur
> Over your threshold: monies is your suit.
> What should I say to you? Should I not say,
> 'Hath a dog money? Is it possible
> A cur can lend three thousand ducats?' or
> Shall I bend low, and in a bondman's key,
> With 'bated breath and whisp'ring humbleness,
> Say this:—
> 'Fair sir, you spet on me Wednesday last;
> You spurn'd me such a day; another time
> You call'd me dog; and for these courtesies
> I'll lend you this much moneys?' "

Antonio replies:

> "I am as like to call thee so again,
> To spit on thee again, to spurn thee too."

Where in all this do you find Christian love? Truly, Shakespeare would have been writing against Christianity, if he had let it be embodied in these characters who are hostile to Shylock, and yet are hardly worthy of untying shoelaces. Bankrupt Antonio is a nerveless creature, without energy, without strength to hate, and hence also without strength to love, a gloomy insect-heart, whose flesh really is good for nothing but "to bait fish withal."

He does not dream of returning the borrowed three thousand ducats to the Jew. Nor does Bassanio repay him. This fellow is, in the words of an English critic, a "genuine fortune hunter"; he borrows money to make sumptuous display so as to bag a rich wife and a fat dowry—for, as he tells his friend:

> " 'Tis not unknown to you, Antonio,
> How much I have disabled mine estate,
> By something showing a more swelling port
> Than any faint means would grant continuance:
> Nor do I now make moan to be abridg'd
> From such a noble rate; but my chief care
> Is, to come fairly off from the great debts
> Wherein my time, something too prodigal,
> Hath left me gag'd. To you, Antonio,
> I owe the most, in money and in love;
> And from your love I have a warranty
> To unburthen all my plots and purposes,
> How to get clear of all the debts I owe."

As for Lorenzo, he is the accomplice of a most heinous theft, and under the Prussian Criminal Code would be sentenced to fifteen years at hard labor, branded and pilloried—although he is not only susceptible to stolen ducats and jewels, but to the beauties of nature as well, moon-lit landscapes and music. As for the other noble Venetians, who appear as Antonio's companions, they do not seem to have any particular aversion to money, either. For their poor friend who has fallen upon evil days they have nothing but words, or "coined air." On that point, our good pious friend, Franz Horn, makes the following thin, but proper remark: "Here one might fairly inquire: How was it possible that Antonio's troubles became so great? All Venice knew and esteemed him; his close friends knew all about the terrible bond, and that the Jew would not abate a tittle of it. Yet they let one day after another pass, until finally the three months are gone, and with them all hopes of rescue. Surely it would have been a simple thing for those good friends, of whom the royal merchant seemed to have such a multitude about him, to raise three thousand ducats to save a life—and what a life!—but such things are always somewhat inconvenient, and so the dear good friends, because they are only so-called friends, or if you will, only half or three-quarter friends,—do nothing, nothing at all, and again nothing. They pity the excellent merchant, who in the past tendered them such fine feasts, but with exceedingly appropriate complacence, they revile Shylock to their hearts' and tongues' content, which also can be done without danger; and then they presume that they have done all that friendship demands. Much as we must hate Shylock, we can hardly blame him for somewhat despising these people, which he probably does. In the end, he seems to confuse Gratiano—whom his absence excuses—with the others and puts him in the same class, by dismissing his earlier inaction and his present flow of words with the cutting remark:

"Till thou canst rail the seal from off my bond,
Thou but offend'st thy lungs to speak so loud:

Repair thy wit, good youth, or it will fall
To cureless ruin.—I stand here for law. "

Or should perhaps Launcelot Gobbo be considered the representative of Christianity? Singularly enough, Shakespeare nowhere expressed himself so clearly about him as in a conversation between this rogue and his mistress. To Jessica's remark, "I shall be saved by my husband; he hath made me a Christian," Launcelot Gobbo replies:

> "Truly, the more to blame he: we were Christians enow before; e'en as many as could well live, one by another. This making of Christians will raise the price of hogs; if we grow all to be pork-eaters, we shall not shortly have a rasher on the coals for money."

Truly, except for Portia, Shylock is the most respectable character in the entire play. He loves money; he does not conceal this love, but cries it aloud in the market-place. But there is something he esteems above money—satisfaction for his injured feelings—just retribution for unspeakable insults; and though offered ten times the loan, he refuses, and does not rue the three thousand or ten times the three thousand ducats, so long as he can buy a pound of the flesh of his enemy's heart. "Thou wilt not take his flesh: what's that good for?" Salarino asks him. And he replies:

> "To bait fish withal: if it will feed nothing else, it will feed my revenge. He hath disgraced me, and hindered me of half a million, laughed at my losses, mocked at my gains, scorned my nation, thwarted my bargains, cooled my friends, heated mine enemies; and what's his reason? I am a Jew. Hath not a Jew eyes? hath not a Jew hands, organs, dimensions, senses, affections, passions? fed with

the same food, hurt with the same weapons,
subject to the same diseases, healed by the same
means, warmed and cooled by the same winter and
summer, as a Christian is? If you prick us, do we
not bleed? if you tickle us, do we not laugh? if you
poison us, do we not die? and if you wrong us, shall
we not revenge? If we are like you in the rest, we
will resemble you in that. If a Jew wrong a
Christian, what is his humility? Revenge. If a
Christian wrong a Jew, what should his sufferance
be by Christian example? Why, revenge. The
villany you teach me, I will execute; and it shall go
hard but I will better the instruction."

No, though Shylock loves money, there are things he
loves far more—among them his daughter, "Jessica, my
child." Though in the great heat of passion he curses her
and would like to see her dead at his feet, with the jewels in
her ears and with the ducats in her coffin, he still loves her
more than all the ducats and jewels. Excluded from public
life and Christian society, and thrust back into the narrow
confines of domestic felicity, the poor Jew has nothing but
family sentiments; and they manifest themselves in him
with the most touching tenderness. The turquoise ring
which his wife Leah once gave him, he would not exchange
for "a wilderness of monkeys." In the court scene, when
Bassanio tells Antonio:

"Antonio, I am married to a wife
Which is as dear to me as life itself;
But life itself, my wife, and all the world,
Are not with me esteem'd above thy life:
I would lose all, ay, sacrifice them all
Here to this devil, to deliver you,"

and Gratiano adds:

> "I have a wife, whom, I protest, I love:
> I would she were in heaven, so she could
> Entreat some power to change this currish Jew."

sudden terror grips Shylock concerning the fate of his daughter, who married among men who are capable of sacrificing their wives for their friends, and aside, but not aloud, he says to himself:

> "These be Christian husbands! I have a daughter
> Would any of the stock of Barrabas
> Had been her husband, rather than a Christian!"

This passage—these whispered words—lay the foundation for the sentence of condemnation which we must pass on fair Jessica. It was no harsh father whom she left, robbed, and betrayed. Shameful betrayal! She even makes common cause with Shylock's enemies, and when they say all sorts of evil things of him at Belmont, Jessica does not cast down her eyes, her lips do not blanch; no, she herself says the worst things about her father. . . Vile outrage! She has no feelings, only a lust for adventure. She is bored in the closely confined "honest" house of the embittered Jew, which finally seems hell to her. Her frivolous heart is too strongly drawn by the lively sounds of the drum and the bent-pipes. Did Shakespeare intend to portray a Jewess here? Certainly not. He only describes a daughter of Eve—one of those pretty birds that fly as soon as they are fledged from the paternal nest to their dear little males. Thus Desdemona followed the Moor; thus Imogene followed Posthumus. This is the way of woman.

In Jessica we may especially note a certain timid shame which she cannot overcome when she puts on a boy's clothes. In this trait, we may perhaps recognize that peculiar chastity which is characteristic of her people, and which lends such a wonderful attraction to their daughters. The chastity of the Jews may have its origin in the opposition which they always maintained against that Oriental worship of senses and sensuality, which once flourished so prolifically among their neighbors, the Egyptians, Phoenicians, Assyrians and Babylonians, and which in continually transformed shapes has survived to this day. The Jews are a chaste, temperate, I might almost say, an abstract people, and in the purity of their morals they stand closest to the Germanic tribes. The modesty of Jewish and Germanic women may not have an absolute value, but in its manifestations it makes a most charming, attractive and touching impression. One is moved to tears to read how after the defeat of the Cimbri and the Teutons, for instance, their women implored Marius not to give them to his soldiers as slaves, but to the priestesses of Vesta.

Striking, indeed, is the deep affinity which prevails between these two ethical nations, Jews and old Germans. This affinity had its source not in history—it was not due, for example, to the fact that the Bible, the great family chronicle of the Jews, served as a textbook for the whole Germanic world; nor to the fact that from the earliest times the Jews and Germans were the most implacable foes of the Romans, hence natural allies. It has a more profound source. Fundamentally, the two peoples are alike—so much alike, that one might regard the Palestine of the past as an Oriental Germany—just as one might regard the Germany of today as the home of the Holy Word, the mother-soil of prophecy, the citadel of pure spirituality.

But it is not Germany alone which possesses the features of Palestine. The rest of Europe too raises itself to the level of the Jews. I say raises itself—for even in the beginning the

Jews bore within them the modern principles which only now are visibly unfolding among the nations of Europe.

Greeks and Romans clung passionately to the soil, to their native land. The later Nordic immigrants into the Greek and Roman world attached themselves to the persons of their chiefs, and ancient patriotism was in the Middle Ages replaced by the fealty of vassals and allegiance to princes. The Jews, however, always clung to the Law, to the abstract idea,—like our own recent cosmopolitan republicans, who regard neither fatherland nor the person of their princes, but rather the law as the highest principle. Yes, cosmopolitanism has sprung almost completely from Judea's soil, and Christ, who was really a Jew, actually founded the propaganda of cosmopolitanism. As for the republicanism of the Jews, I recall having read in Josephus that there were republicans in Jerusalem who opposed the royalist Herodians, fought against them very courageously, called no man their lord, and bitterly hated Roman absolutism. Their religion was freedom and equality. What a chimaera!

But in the last analysis what is the cause of that hatred between the followers of the Mosaic law and those of the teachings of Christ, which we see in Europe to the present day, and of which the poet, by illustrating the universal through the particular, gave us so gruesome a picture in *The Merchant of Venice?* Is it the primordial brother-hatred, caused by differences in divine worship, which we see soon after the Creation, erupting between Cain and Abel? Or is religion on the whole only a pretext, and men hate each other for the sake of hatred, just as they love each other for the sake of love? Which side is to blame for this rancor? In trying to answer this question, I feel I must include a passage from a private letter, which does full justice to Shylock's enemies, too:

"I do not condemn the hatred with which the common people persecute the Jews. I only condemn the unfortunate errors which gave birth to that hatred. The people are always right in this matter. Their hatred as well as their love is always based on a perfectly sound instinct; but they do not know how to formulate their sentiments correctly, and instead of issues, their wrath is usually directed against persons—the innocent scapegoats of temporary or local maladjustments. The people suffer want, they are deprived of the means of enjoying life, and though the priests of the state religions assure them that 'man is here on earth to practice self-denial and to obey the authorities despite hunger and thirst,' the people secretly long for the means of enjoyment, and hate those in whose chests and vaults such means are accumulated. They hate the rich and are happy if religion allows them to give vent to this hatred without restraint. The common people always hated in the Jews only the possessors of money; it was always the heaped-up metal which drew down the lightning of their wrath on the Jews. The spirit of each age merely gives an appropriate slogan to this hatred. Thus, in the Middle Ages, that slogan wore the dark colors of the Catholic Church, and the Jews were murdered and plundered because "they crucified Christ"—with the very same logic employed by certain black Christians in San Domingo, who, at the times of the massacres, ran about with a picture of the Saviour on the cross and shrieked fanatically: '*Les blancs l'ont tué, tuons tous les blancs!*'

"My friend, you laugh at the poor Negroes. I assure you that the West Indian planters did not laugh then; they were butchered in expiation of Christ exactly like the Jews of Europe a few centuries before. But the black Christians in San Domingo were also right in this matter. The whites lived idly, in the full enjoyment of all pleasures, while the Negroes had to slave for them in the sweat of their black brows, and as wages received nothing but a little rice and very many strokes of the lash. The blacks were the common people.

"We are no longer living in the Middle Ages. The common people, too, are growing more enlightened. They no longer kill Jews on sight—they no longer extenuate their hatred with religion. Our age is no longer so naively bigoted; the traditional animus is cloaked in more modern phrases, and in the beer halls as well as in the chambers of deputies the mob declaims against the Jews with economic, industrial, scientific, even philosophic arguments. Only hardened hypocrites still give their hatred a religious coloring and persecute the Jews for the sake of Christ. The great majority openly admit that material interests are really at stake, and seek by all means to obstruct the Jews in the full exercise of their industrial capacities. Here in Frankfurt, for example, only twenty-four adherents of the Mosaic faith may marry each year, lest the population multiply excessively and there be too much competition for the Christian tradespeople. Here the true reason for anti-Semitism emerges with its real face; no longer with the gloomy, fanatical monkish mien, but with the flabby enlightened features of a shopkeeper afraid of being outdone in business dealings by Jewish business sense.

"But is it the fault of the Jews that this business sense has developed in them in so menacing a form? It is entirely the fault of that madness with which the people of the Middle Ages ignored the importance of industry, regarded trade as ignoble, and money transactions as particularly shameful; and thus turned over the most profitable of these industrial enterprises—the business of money—to the Jews. Since these were barred from all other trades, they perforce became the shrewdest merchants and bankers. The world compelled them to become rich, and then hated them for their riches; and although Christendom has now dropped its prejudices against industry, and in trade and industry Christians have become as knavish as the Jews, and as rich, the traditional hatred of the masses has clung to the Jews, and they still see in them the representatives of money and hate them for it. You see, in world history, everyone is right—the hammer as well as the anvil."

Hebrew Melodies

BY HEINRICH HEINE

Translated into English by Hal Draper

Heinrich Heine in 1847

Oh, let your life not drain to an end
  Without tasting life's treasure!
And when you're safely sheltered, friend,
  Let them shoot at their pleasure.

If happiness should pass your way,
  Then seize it—don't dally.
Don't build your hut on a hilltop, I say,
  But down in the valley.

PRINCESS SABBATH

In Arabia's book of fables
We can see enchanted princes
Who at times regain their former
Human shape and comely figure:

Once again the hairy monster
Changes back into a princeling,
Dressed in brightly jeweled splendor,
Sweetly fluting amorous ditties.

But the magic respite ends,
And again all of a sudden
We behold his royal highness
Retransmuted to a monster.

Of a prince so used by fortune
Is the song I sing. His name is
Israel. A witch's magic
Has transformed him to a dog.

5   As a dog with doggish notions,
All the livelong week he piddles
Through life's slime and slops and sweepings,
Mocked and jeered at by street-arabs.

But on every Friday evening
At the twilight hour, the magic
Fades abruptly, and the dog
Once more is a human being.

Human now, with human feelings,
Head and heart uplifted proudly,
Dressed in clean and festive clothing,
He goes in his father's mansion.

"Greetings to you, cherished mansion
Of my noble lord and father!
Tents of Jacob, see, I kiss your
Holy doorposts with my lips!"

Through the house a mystic stir
And mysterious whispers vibrate,
And the house's unseen master
Breathes into the awe-filled silence.

10   Silence! Just the sacristan
(*Vulgo* synagogue attendant)
Scurries here and there and briskly
Gets the evening lamps all lighted.

Golden lights that promise solace,
How they glow, oh how they glimmer!
Flaring candles flicker proudly
From the railing of the pulpit.

By the ark that holds the Torah
And that's overhung with costly
Panoplies of silken covers,
Sparkling bright with precious jewels—

There, behind his prayer table
Stands the congregation's cantor—
Dapper little man who shoulders
His black cloak coquettishly.

To display how white his hand is,
With his neck he fidgets oddly,
Index finger pressed to temple,
Thumb reposing on the throat line.

15   First he hums it very softly
To himself, until at last he
Sings out loud in exultation:
"L'khah dodi likras kallah!"

"L'khah dodi likras kallah—
Come, my love, the bride awaits you,
Waits already to uncover
Blushing visage to your eyes!"

This delightful nuptial song was
Written by the great and glorious,
Celebrated minnesinger,
Don Jehuda ben Halevy.

In the song he sings to honor
Nuptial rites of Israel
With the lady Princess Sabbath,
Who is called the silent princess.

Pearl of beauty, flower of beauty
Is the princess. Not more lovely
Was the famous Queen of Sheba,
Bosom friend of Solomon,

20   Ethiopian bluestocking,
        Who would use her wit to dazzle,
        But whose clever riddles ended
        By becoming merely tiresome.

        Princess Sabbath, who indeed is
        Restfulness and calm incarnate,
        Loathes all manner of polemics
        And all forms of disputation.

        Equally unpleasant to her
        Is the roar of ranting passion
        Or the shriek of empty pathos
        With disheveled hair aflutter.

        Modestly the silent princess
        Hides her braids inside her bonnet—
        Eyes like young gazelles and softer,
        Blooming like a slender myrtle.

        She allows all to her lover,
        All except tobacco-smoking:
        "Darling, smoking is forbidden,
        Since today's the Sabbath day.

        "But instead you will, at midday,
        Get a dish steamed up to please you,
        A divinely tasty morsel—
        You will feast today on schalet!"

        Schalet, shining gleam from Heaven,
        Daughter of Elysium!—
        Schiller's ode would sound like this if
        He had ever tasted schalet.

        Schalet is the food of Heaven,
        And the recipe was given
        By the Lord himself to Moses
        One fine day upon Mount Sinai,

On the very spot where likewise
God revealed his moral doctrines
And the holy Ten Commandments
In the midst of flames and lightning.

Schalet is God's bread of rapture,
It's the kosher-type ambrosia
That is catered straight from Heaven;
And compared with such a morsel

30   The ambrosia of the pagan
Pseudogods of ancient Hellas,
Who were devils in disguise, is
Just a pile of devils' *dreck*.

Feasting on such fare, the prince is
As transfigured, eyes aglowing,
Hands unbuttoning his waistcoat;
And with blissful smiles he murmurs:

"Don't I hear the Jordan plashing?
Is it not the fountains spraying
In the palmy vale of Bethel
Where the camels rest from labor?

"Don't I hear the sheep bells tinkling?
Is it not the fatted wethers
That the shepherd drives at evening
Down from Gilead's high pastures?"

But the lovely day is dimming;
Striding on long legs of shadow
Comes the evil hour of magic—
And the prince lets out a sigh.

35   It's as if the ice-cold fingers
Of a witch had clutched his heartstrings.
Shivers rippling through him herald
The old dog-transfiguration.

Then the princess gives her golden
Spicebox to the prince, and slowly
He inhales—once more regaling
All his senses with the fragrance.

And the princess also offers
Next the parting cup to drink from—
Hastily he drinks it, leaving
Just a few drops in the goblet.

These he sprinkles on the table,
Then he takes a small wax taper
And he dips it in the moisture
Till it crackles and goes out.

JEHUDA BEN HALEVY

i
"Dry with thirst, oh let my tongue cleave
To my palate—let my right hand
Wither off, if I forget thee
Ever, O Jerusalem—"

Words and melody keep buzzing
In my head today, unceasing,
And I seem to make out voices
Singing psalms, I hear men's voices——

Sometimes, too, I catch a glimpse of
Shadowy long beards in darkness—
Phantom figures, which of you
Is Jehuda ben Halevy?

But they scurry by me quickly—
Ghosts will shun with fear the clumsy
Consolations of the living—
Yet I recognized him there—

5   I could recognize his pallid
Forehead, proudly worn with thinking,
And his eyes, so gentle-stubborn—
Pained, inquiring eyes that pierce me—

But I recognized him mostly
By his enigmatic way of
Smiling with those rhyming lips,
Which are found in poets only.

Years come round and years go fleeting.
Since Jehuda ben Halevy
Saw the light, the world has counted
Seven hundred years and fifty;

It was in Castile's Toledo
That he came into the world,
And the golden Tagus crooned him
Lullabies beside the cradle.

His strict father early nurtured
His development and thinking,
And his education started
With the book of God, the Torah.

10   And the youngster read this volume
In the ancient text, whose lovely
Picturesquely hieroglyphic
Old Chaldean squared-off letters

Are derived out of the childhood
Of the world, and for this reason
Show familiar, smiling features
To all childlike minds and spirits.

This authentic ancient text
Was recited by the youngster
In the old, original singsong
Known as *Tropp* down through the ages—

And with loving care he gurgled
Those fat gutterals right gladly,
And the quaver, the Shalsheleth,
He trilled like a feathered warbler.

As for Onkelos's Targum,
Which is written in that special
Low-Judaic idiom
That we call the Aramaic

15   And which bears the same relation
To the language of the prophets
That the Swabian has to German—
In this garlic-sausage Hebrew

Was the boy instructed likewise,
And this knowledge soon provided
Solid service to his efforts
In the study of the Talmud.

Yes, his father early led him
To the pages of the Talmud,
And thereby he laid before him
The Halacha, that prodigious

School of fencing, where the greatest
Of the dialectic athletes
In the Babylonian contests
Used to carry on their war games.

Here the boy could master every
Art and science of polemic;
And his mastery was later
Witnessed by his book *Kuzari*.

20   But the heavens shed upon us
      Two quite different kinds of luster:
      There's the sun's harsh-glaring daylight
      And the milder moonlight—likewise,

      Likewise, shining in the Talmud
      Is a double light, divided
      In Halacha and Haggada.
      Fencing school I called the former,

      But the latter, the Haggada,
      I would rather call a garden,
      A phantasmagoric garden
      That is very like another

      That once bloomed and sprouted also
      From the soil of Babylonia—
      Queen Semiramis' great garden,
      That eighth wonder of the world.

      Queen Semiramis was brought up
      As a child by birds, and always
      Later on retained a number
      Of their birdlike traits and temper,

25   And so she refused to walk on
      Lowly ground like common mammals
      And insisted on the planting
      Of a garden in the air:—

      Rising high on giant pillars
      Cypresses and palm trees flourished,
      Orange trees and beds of flowers,
      Marble statues, even fountains,

      All secured with cunning braces
      Formed by countless hanging bridges,
      Made to look like vines and creepers,
      On which birds would swing and teeter—

Big and bright-hued birds, deep thinkers
Much too solemn-faced to warble,
While around them fluttered bands of
Little finches, gaily trilling.

All of them were blithely breathing
Air distilled of balsam fragrance,
Unpolluted by the reek of
Earth's miasma and malodors.

30   The Haggada is a garden
Of such childlike airy fancy.
And the young Talmudic scholar—
When his heart felt dry and dusty,

Musty from the noisy squabbling
Over the Halacha, over
Quarrels on the plaguy egg
That a hen laid on a feast day,

Or about some other question
Equally profound—the youngster
Fled for solace of the spirit
To the blossom-filled Haggada,

With its lovely olden fables,
Tales of angels, myths and legends,
Tranquil stories of the martyrs,
Festive songs and wise old sayings,

Droll exaggerations also,
Yet it all had faith's old power,
Faith's old fire—Oh, how it sparkled,
Bubbling with exuberance—

35   And the youngster's noble spirit
Was enraptured by the sweetness
Wild and wonderful adventure,
And the strangely aching gladness,

And the fabled thrills and shivers
Of that blissful secret world,
Of that mighty revelation
Which we title poesy.

And the art of poesy—
Gaia scienza, gracious talent
That we call the poet's art—
Also worked upon his spirit.

Thus Jehuda ben Halevy
Grew to be not just a scholar
But a master of poetics
And a great and mighty poet.

Yes, he was a mighty poet,
Star and beacon for his age,
Light and lamp among his people,
And a wonderful and mighty

40 Pillar of poetic fire
In the vanguard of all Israel's
Caravan of woe and sorrow
In the desert waste of exile.

Pure and truthful, without blemish,
Was his song—his soul was also.
On the day his Maker fashioned
This great soul, He paused contented,

Kissed the soul whose beauty sparkled;
And those kisses still go thrilling
Through the poet's every measure
Hallowed by this grace and bounty.

Both in poetry and life,
It's the gift of grace that governs—
He who has this highest good can
Never sin in prose or verse.

Any poet who possesses
This, God's grace, we call a genius:
Monarch in the realm of thought, he
Is responsible to no man.

45   He accounts to God, God only,
Not the people; both in art
And in life, the people can
Kill us but can never judge us.

ii
"By the Babylonian waters
There we sat and wept—our harps were
Hung upon the weeping willow . . ."
That old song—do you still know it?

That old tune—do you still know it?—
How it starts with elegiac
Whining, humming like a kettle
That is seething on the hearth?

Long has it been seething in me—
For a thousand years. Black sorrow!
And my wounds are licked by time
Just as Job's dog licked his boils.

Dog, I thank you for your spittle,
But its coolness merely soothes me—
Only death can really heal me,
But, alas, I am immortal!

5   Years come round and years pass onward—
In the loom the spool is whirring,
Busy flying hither-thither—
What it weaves no weaver knows.

Years come round and years pass onward,
And men's teardrops trickle slowly

Into earth, and earth absorbs them
In a dark and greedy silence—

Seething mad! The lid blows off—
Hail to him, the man "that taketh
All thy little ones and dasheth
This young brood against the stones."

God be thanked! the steam is cooling
In the kettle, which now slowly
Quiets down. My spleen subsides,
That black Western-Eastern spleen—

And my winged horse is neighing,
Glad once more, and seems to shake off
Baleful nightmares from his spirit,
And his knowing eyes are asking:

10   "Shouldn't we go back to Spain now,
To the young Talmudic scholar
Who became a mighty poet—
To Jehuda ben Halevy?"

Yes, he did become a great one,
Sovereign ruler of the dream world,
Monarch of the mind and spirit,
Poet by God's grace and bounty,

Who, in God-imbued *sirventes*,
Madrigals and sweet terzinas,
Canzonets and sultry ghazels,
Poured out incandescent ardors

From his God-kissed soul and spirit!
Yes indeed, this troubadour
Was the equal of the greatest
Lutanists in old Provence,

In Poitou, or in Guienne,
Roussillon, or all the other
Lovely lands of orange blossoms
Of our gallant Christendom.

15   Ah, our gallant Christendom's
Lovely lands of orange blossoms!
Ah, how fragrant, shining, plangent
In the twilight of remembrance!

Lovely world of nightingales!
Where men worshiped not the true God
But the false god Love, him only,
And bowed down before the Muses.

Clerics, with their wreaths of roses
On bald pates, sang psalms and hymnals
In the blithe tongue of Provence;
And the noble knights, the laymen,

Trotted proud on lofty chargers,
Mulling over rhymes and verses
Made in honor of the ladies
Whom they served with jocund hearts.

There's no love without a lady,
And a lady was essential
To a troubadour, like butter
To a piece of bread and butter.

20   So too he, the hero sung here,
So Jehuda ben Halevy
Had a ladylove he honored—
But she was a special case.

She was not another Laura,
Whose sweet eyes—those mortal starlets—
On Good Friday in the duomo
Lit a blaze now celebrated;

She was no chatelaine, presiding
In the flower of youth and beauty
Over tournaments and jousting,
Handing out the knightly laurels;

Nor a casuist who lectured
On the legal code of kissing
Or some other law or dogma
In a learned Court of Love.

She, the rabbi's love, was just a
Sad and wretched little darling,
Woeful image of destruction—
She was named Jerusalem.

25   Even in his early childhood
She had all his love already,
And his heart already quivered
At the word Jerusalem.

Then the boy would stand and listen,
Scarlet flames on cheeks, when pilgrims
Journeyed through Toledo coming
From a far-off Eastern country,

And told people how defiled and
Devastated were the places
Where the soil still glowed with radiance
From the footsteps of the prophets,

Where the air was still imbued with
The eternal breath of God—
"What a lamentable sight!" once
Cried a pilgrim, whose long beard

Flowed down silver-white, though strangely
At its tip the hair was growing
Black again, and almost seemed to
Undergo rejuvenation—

30   Yes, a curious-looking pilgrim
      Must this man have been, whose eyes
      Held a thousand years of sorrow;
      And he sighed, "Jerusalem!"

      "She, the crowded holy city,
      Has become a desolation
      Where wood demons, werewolves, jackals
      Carry on their vile existence—

      "Snakes and birds of night are nesting
      In its mouldering walls and ramparts;
      From the windows' airy arches
      Foxes gaze in carefree comfort.

      "Here and there one sometimes glimpses
      Ragged peons of the desert
      Letting their old humpbacked camels
      Pasture on tall-growing grasses.

      "On the noble heights of Zion
      Where the golden stronghold towered
      Whose majestic splendor witnessed
      To the great king's pomp and glory—

35   "There the weeds grow rank and only
      Gray old ruins still are standing,
      Looking so forlorn and woeful
      One might fancy they were weeping.

      "And it's said they really do weep
      One day every year, upon the
      Ninth day of the month of Ab—
      I myself, with hot eyes streaming,

      "Saw the heavy teardrops seeping
      Slowly from the mighty stone blocks,
      And I heard the lamentations
      Of the broken temple pillars."—

Stories from such pious pilgrims
Wakened in the youthful bosom
Of Jehuda ben Halevy
Yearnings for Jerusalem.

Poets' yearnings! dreamy bodings,
Ominous as was the longing
That once at his Chateau Blaye
Filled the noble-souled Vidame,

40   Noble troubadour Rudel,
When—to knights who had returned from
Eastern lands, midst clinking goblets—
He presented this assertion:

"Paragon of grace and breeding,
Pearl and flower of all women
Is the lovely Melisande,
Tripoli's enchanting countess."

Everyone knows that this lady
Was the troubadour's belovèd,
That he sang her praise, and felt that
Chateau Blaye was cramped and straitened.

Longing drove him forth. At Cette
He took ship, but on the water
He fell sick, and, close to dying,
Made his way to Tripoli.

Here he saw his Melisande;
Finally his eyes beheld her
But that selfsame hour the shadow
Of grim death closed them forever.

45   Thus he sang his final love-song,
And he died there at the feet of
Melisande, his longed-for lady,
Tripoli's enchanting countess.

Wonderful is the resemblance
In the fate of these two poets!
Save that one was in his old age
When he launched his pilgrimage.

And Jehuda ben Halevy
Also died at his love's feet,
And his dying head lay resting
On Jerusalem's fair knees.

iii
When the battle of Arbela
Ended, Alexander took the
Lands and peoples of Darius,
Court and harem, horses, women,

Elephants and jingling darics,
Crown and scepter—golden rubbish—
And he stuck it all into his
Baggy Macedonian breeches.

In the tent of great Darius,
Who had fled lest he himself be
Stuck away with other booty,
Our young hero found a casket.

This small golden chest was graced with
Miniatures and filagree work
And was splendidly adorned with
Cameos and crusted jewels.

5   Now, this chest, itself a treasure
Of inestimable value,
Served to hold the monarch's treasures,
All his precious body jewels.

Alexander gave these jewels
To brave soldiers in his army,
Smiling at the thought that men get
Childlike joy from colored pebbles.

One rich jewel of the fairest
He sent to his cherished mother;
Once the signet ring of Cyrus,
It was now set in a brooch.

And he sent to Aristotle,
Teacher and the world's rump-thumper,
A big onyx for his noted
Natural history collection.

Also in the chest were pearls,
Strung into a wondrous necklace,
Which were once to Queen Atossa
Given by the bogus Smerdis;

10 But the pearls themselves were real—
And the gleeful victor gave them
To a beauty of a dancer,
Come from Corinth, name of Thaïs.

Thaïs wore them in her tresses,
Which streamed loose like a bacchante,
On the night of fire when, dancing
At Persepolis, she boldly

Flung her torch at the king's castle,
So that flames shot up and crackled
In a noisy conflagration
Like the fireworks on a feast-day.

On the death of lovely Thaïs—
Which took place in Babylon
Of a Babylonian ailment—
The pearl necklace was disposed of

At a local public auction.
There a priest from Memphis bought them,
Took them on to Egypt, where they
Turned up somewhat later, on

15   Cleopatra's dressing table;
She then crushed the finest pearl and
Mixed it into wine and drank it,
Just to chaff Mark Antony.

With the last of the Omayyads
Came this string of pearls to Spain,
And they coiled it round the turban
Of the Caliph in Cordova.

Abderam the Third then wore it
As his favor at the tourney
Where he pierced the thirty golden
Circlets and Zuleima's heart.

With the Moorish empire's downfall
The pearl necklace also passed on
To the Christians, and it wound up
In the crown jewels of Castile.

Their most Catholic Majesties, the
Queens of Spain, adorned their persons
With the pearls on court occasions,
Plays and bullfights and processions,

20   And at auto-da-fés also,
Where on balconies in comfort
They regaled themselves with fragrant
Whiffs of old Jews slowly roasting.

Later on, the son of Satan,
Mendizábal, put these pearls
Out to pawn, to cover certain
Deficits in state finances.

At the Tuileries the necklace
Showed up for its last appearance,
Shimmering on the neck of Madame
Solomon, the baroness.

So it went with these fine pearls.
Less adventurous was the story
Of the casket: Alexander
Kept it for his very own.

In it he enclosed the poems
That ambrosial Homer chanted,
Favorites of his; at nighttime
At the head of his hard pallet

25   Stood the chest; while he lay sleeping
Radiant forms of heroes rose up
From the casket and they drifted
Into Alexander's dreams.

Other times, and other birds—
I too once loved just as keenly
All those songs about the deeds of
Great Achilles and Odysseus.

In those days my heart was sunny
And the world shot through with crimson,
And my brow was wreathed in vine leaves,
And the air was filled with fanfares—

Hush, enough!—all smashed to pieces
Is my proud triumphal chariot,
And the panthers that once drew it
Are all dead—likewise the women

Who, with drums and cymbals clashing,
Danced about me; I myself
Writhe here on the ground in torment,
Cripple's torment—hush, enough!—

30   Hush, enough!—our story's subject
        Is the casket of Darius.
        In my own mind I was thinking:
        If I ever owned that casket

        And were not compelled to sell it
        Right away for ready money,
        I would keep enclosed within it
        All the poems of our rabbi—

        All Jehuda ben Halevy's
        Festal songs and lamentations,
        Madrigals and travel pictures
        Of his pilgrimage—I'd have it

        All engrossed on purest parchment
        By the greatest scribe that's living,
        And I'd place this manuscript in
        That same golden little casket.

        I would put it on a table
        At the head of my hard pallet,
        And when friends came round and marveled
        At the little box's splendors,

35   At the bas-relief's rare beauty,
        So minute and yet so perfect
        Both at once, and at the size of
        The encrusted precious jewels—

        Smiling then I'd tell them: This is
        Nothing but the roughhewn shell that
        Holds the greater treasure in it—
        Here within this chest are lying

        Diamonds whose radiant luster
        Is the mirror of the heavens,
        Rubies burning red as heart's blood,
        Turquoises of flawless beauty,

Emeralds of glowing promise—
Yes, and pearls of purer water
Than were once to Queen Atossa
Given by the bogus Smerdis,

Or than those that later shimmered
On a host of noted figures
Of this moon-encircled planet—
Thaïs, say, or Cleopatra,

40   Priests of Isis, Moorish princes,
Queens of Spain and other monarchs,
And at last the worthy Madame
Solomon, the baroness—

These world-famous pearls are merely
Whitish slime secretions from a
Hapless oyster lying sea-deep
Suffering from some stupid ailment;

But the pearls within this casket
Are the lovely product of a
Beauty-mantled human soul that's
Deeper than the ocean chasms;

For they are the teardrop pearls that
Once Jehuda ben Halevy
Let fall over the destruction
Of his love, Jerusalem—

Pearly teardrops, strung together
By a golden thread of verses,
Made into a song by labors
In the poet's golden forge.

45   This, his song of pearly teardrops,
Is the famous lamentation
Sung in all the tents of Jacob,
Scattered far through all the world,

On the ninth day of the month that's
Known as Ab, the year's remembrance
Of Jerusalem's destruction
By Vespasian's scion Titus.

Yes, it is the song of Zion,
Which Jehuda ben Halevy
Sang amid the holy ruins
Of Jerusalem, and died.

Clad in penitential raiment
He sat barefoot on the fragment
Of a crumbling fallen column;
Flowing down upon his bosom

Like a gray wildwood his tresses
Cast fantastic shadows over
His pale face where anguish peered out
Like a ghost from haunted eyes.

50   Thus he sat and sang; he seemed like
Some old prophet of past ages,
Just as if old Jeremiah
Had arisen from the graveyard.

Even birds around the ruins,
Hearing his wild song of anguish,
Were made tame—the vultures listened
And approached, as in compassion—

But a Saracen came riding
Brazen-souled along the roadway;
Rocking back high on his charger,
Down he swung a shining lance

Into the poor singer's bosom,
And the deadly shaft was fatal;
Then he rode off at a gallop
Like a shape of wingèd shadow.

Tranquil flowed the rabbi's lifeblood,
Tranquilly he sang his song out
To the end, and his last dying
Sigh breathed out: Jerusalem!—

55   There's an ancient legend stating
That the Saracen was really
Not an evil human being
But an angel in disguise,

Sent from Heaven to deliver
God's own favorite from this world,
And to expedite his painless
Passage to the Blessèd Kingdom.

Up above, it states, a special
Flattering reception waited
To accord the poet honor—
What a heavenly surprise!

Festively a choir of angels
Came to greet him playing music,
And the hymn he heard in welcome
Was a poem of his own—

His own Sabbath hymeneal,
Synagogal nuptial song,
With the well-known merry-lilting
Melodies—what strains of gladness!

60   Little angels blew on oboes,
Little angels played the fiddle,
Others strummed upon violas,
Beat the drum or clashed the cymbals.

And it all went ringing, singing,
Sweetly echoing through the distant
Spaces of the realm of Heaven:
"L'khah dodi likras kallah."

iv
My good wife's dissatisfaction
With the chapter just concluded
Bears especially upon the
Precious casket of Darius.

Almost bitterly she comments
That a husband who was truly
So religious would have cashed in
The old casket on the instant,

And would certainly have purchased
For his lawful wedded wife
The fine cashmere shawl she needed
With such monumental urgence.

And Jehuda ben Halevy,
In her view, would have been honored
Quite enough by being kept in
Any pretty box of cardboard

5   With some very swanky Chinese
Arabesques to decorate it,
Like a bonbon box from Marquis
In the Passage Panorama.

"Strange!" she adds in further comment,
"That I never heard the name of
This great poet that you speak of,
This Jehuda ben Halevy."

And I answered her as follows:—
Dearest child, your lack of knowledge
Is quite sweet, but shows the defects
Of the French-type education

That the boarding schools of Paris
Give to girls, those future mothers

Of a freedom-loving people,
Who are thoroughly instructed

On old mummies, or the pharaohs
Who were stuffed in ancient Egypt,
Merovingian shadow-monarchs,
Or unpowdered wigs on ladies,

10   Or the pigtailed lords of China,
Procelain-pagoda princes—
All of this is crammed into them,
Clever girls! but, oh ye heavens—

If you ask them for great figures
In the golden age of glory
Of the Arabic Hispanic
Jewish school of poetry—

If you ask about the trio
Of Jehuda ben Halevy
And of Solomon Gabirol
And of Moses Ibn Ezra—

If you ask about such figures,
Then the children stare back at you
With their goggling eyes wide open—
Like the cows along a hillside.

I'd advise you, my belovèd,
To make up what you've neglected,
And to learn the Hebrew language;
Drop the theater and concerts,

15   Go devote some years of study
To this subject—you'll be able
To read all of them in Hebrew,
Ibn Ezra and Gabirol

And of course Halevy also—
The triumvirate of song, who
Once evoked the sweetest music
From the harp that David cherished.

Alcharisi—who no doubt you
Also do not know although he
Was a Gallic wag who out-wagged
The *Makamat* of Hariri

And in this department shone as
A Voltairean six hundred
Years before Voltaire was fathered—
This same Alcharisi stated:

"It's through thought Gabirol sparkles
And it's thinkers that he pleases,
Whereas Ibn Ezra sparkles
In his art, and suits the artist—

20   "But Jehuda ben Halevy
Has both qualities together,
And he is a mighty poet
And a favorite of all."

Ibn Ezra was a friend
And I think also a cousin
Of Jehuda ben Halevy;
In his travel book he sadly

Heaps laments that in Granada
He once vainly tried to search out
His good poet-friend, but only
Found his brother, the physician,

Rabbi Meyer, poet also
And the father of a beauty
Who enkindled Ibn Ezra's
Heart with flames of hopeless passion.

To forget his little cousin,
He took pilgrim's staff and wandered
Like so many of his colleagues,
Living vagrantly and homeless.

25   Faring toward Jerusalem,
He was set upon by Tartars,
And they bound him on a horse and
Bore him to their native steppes.

There he had to render service
Hardly worthy of a rabbi
And still less so of a poet—
Namely, he was milking cows.

Once, as he was stiffly squatting
Underneath a cow's big belly,
Busy fingering the udder
To spray milk into the bucket—

An undignified position
For a rabbi or a poet—
Melancholy overwhelmed him
And he sadly starting singing,

And he sang so well and sweetly
That the Khan, the tribal chieftain,
Passing by, was moved to pity,
And he gave the slave his freedom.

30   And he also gave him presents:
A long Saracen mandolin,
One fox pelt, and travel money
To insure his safe return.

What a fate's reserved for poets!
Star of evil, deadly gadfly
Of Apollo's sons, and one that
Did not even spare their father

On that day when, chasing Daphne,
He reached out for her white body
And instead embraced a laurel—
What a big divine Schlemihl!

Yes, the highborn Delphic god is
A Schlemihl; indeed, the laurel
That enwreathes his brow so proudly
Is a sign of this Schlemihldom.

What the word Schlemihl denotes is
Known to us. Long since, Chamisso
Saw to it that it got German
Civic rights—I mean the *word* did.

35   But its origin is still as
Far from known as are the sources
Of the holy Nile; I've pondered
Many a night upon this subject.

Many years ago I traveled
To Berlin to see Chamisso,
Our good friend, for information
From the dean of the Schlemihls.

But he could not satisfy me
And referred me on to Hitzig,
Who had been the first to tell him
What this Peter-without-shadow

Had for surname. So I straightway
Took a droshky and rushed to the
Court Investigator Hitzig,
Who was formerly called Itzig.

Back when he'd been still an Itzig,
He had dreamed a dream in which he
Saw his name inscribed on heaven
With the letter H in front.

40   What did his H mean? he wondered—
       Did it mean perhaps. *Herr* Itzig,
       Holy Itzig (for Saint Itzig)?
       Holy's a fine title—but not

       Suited for Berlin. Brain-weary,
       Finally he made it Hitzig;
       It was only faithful friends who
       Knew a saint hid in the *Hitzig*.

       "Holy Hitzig!" said I, therefore,
       When I saw him, "Kindly tell me
       What the etymology of
       This odd word Schlemihl may be."

       Long the saint talked round the question—
       Couldn't quite remember—piled up
       One excuse upon the other,
       Always Christianlike—until I

       Finally burst all the buttons
       On the breeches of my patience,
       And I started roundly swearing
       With such blasphemies and curses

45   That the godly Pietist,
       Pale as death and knees atrembling,
       Promptly granted what I wanted,
       And this tale is what he told me:

       "In the Bible it is written
       That, while wandering in the desert,
       Often Israel made merry
       With the daughters born of Canaan;

       "So it came to pass that one day
       Phinehas saw noble Zimri
       Fornicating with a woman
       Of the Canaanitish stock,

"And he straightway boiled with anger,
Seized his spear, and thrust it into
Zimri, killing him instanter—
So it tells us in the Bible.

"But the people have a different
Oral version of this story,
Namely, that it was not Zimri
Who was slain by Phinehas,

50   "But that he, made blind by fury,
Unawares struck not the sinner
But an innocent bystander,
One Schlemihl ben Zuri-shaddai."—

Well now, this Schlemihl the First is
Forebear of the race and lineage
Of Schlemihls. We are descended
From Schlemihl ben Zuri-shaddai.

To be sure, we have no mention
Of heroic deeds by this one;
We know only what his name was,
And that he was a Schlemihl.

Still, one's family tree is valued
Not for the good fruit it turns out
But for age—how far it goes back—
Ours can boast three thousand years!

Years come round and years pass onward—
Full three thousand years have fleeted
Since the death of our forebear,
Herr Schlemihl ben Zuri-shaddai.

55   Phinehas is long dead also—
But his spear is ever with us,
And we constantly can hear it
Swishing round above our heads.

And the hearts it smites are noblest—
Like Jehuda ben Halevy's;
It smote Moses Ibn Ezra
And it smote Gabirol also—

Yes, Gabirol, that truehearted
God-enraptured minnesinger,
Pious nightingale who warbled
To the God who was his rose—

That sweet nightingale, who caroled
Tenderly his lilting love songs
In the rayless darkness of the
Gothic medieval night!

Unaffrighted and untroubled
By the goblin shapes and phantoms,
By the maze of death and madness
Haunting us through that long night—

60   That sweet nightingale thought only
Of his heavenly belovèd
Unto whom he sobbed his passion,
Whom his songs of praise exalted!—

Here on earth, Gabirol lived through
Thirty Springs, but Fama's trumpet
Blazoned forth his name and glory
To the people of all nations.

In Cordova, where he dwelt, he
Had a Moor as nearest neighbor
Who wrote verses, too, and so felt
Envy of the poet's fame.

When the poet sang, the Moor was
Filled with rancor on the instant,
For the sweetness of the songs was
Bitter to this jealous grudger.

So he lured the hated poet
To his house by night, and killed him,
And then buried his poor body
In the garden to the rear.

65   But behold, from out the ground where
He'd consigned the corpse to darkness,
There precisely grew a fig tree
Of the most supernal beauty.

All its fruits were strangely long and
Of a strangely spicy sweetness;
All who tasted them were spellbound
In a dreamy haze of rapture.

Whispered talk and muttered rumors
Made the rounds among the people,
Till at last the tittle-tattle
Reached the Caliph's noble ears.

He made use of his own tongue to
Test this fig phenomenon,
And in consequence appointed
A commission of inquiry.

They went straight to work. The owner
Of the tree got sixty lashes
With a cane upon his foot soles,
And confessed the dreadful crime.

70   Thereupon they tore the fig tree,
Roots and all, up from the soil,
And Gabirol's murdered body
Was discovered to the light.

With all pomp they reinterred him,
And his brethren stood in mourning;

On that selfsame day the Moor was
Hanged upon Cordova's gallows.

[*End of fragment*]

DISPUTATION

In the Aula at Toledo
Fanfares blare, the drumbeat rolls;
To a spiritual tourney
Crowds of people swarm in shoals.

It's no secular encounter
With steel sabers, hauberks, heaumes—
Here it's words that are the lances,
And they're honed on learned tomes.

Here the champions serve no lady,
They're not gallant paladins—
On this tilting ground the knights are
Rabbis versus Capuchins.

Not with helmets, but with skullcaps
Or black cowls shall one prevail;
Scapulars and *Arbakanfos*
Form their trusty armored mail.

5   Which is the true God? The Hebrews'—
Stern, unbending, fixed afar,
And all One—whose champion here is
Rabbi Judah of Navarre?

Or perhaps is it the threefold
Christian God of love, instead,

Championed here by Friar José,
The Franciscans' monkish head?

Through the power of cold reason,
Through the links in logic's chain,
And citations from the authors
Whose authority is plain

Will each champion push his rival
Ad absurdum more or less,
And so prove his God is truly
Immanent with godliness.

And whoever is defeated
In this bout, it's specified,
He shall take on the religion
Of his adversary's side;

10   Thus the Jew would take the holy
Sacrament and be baptized,
Or contrariwise the Christian
Would be duly circumcised.

At the side of each contender
Are eleven friends also
Who are bound to share his fortune
Whether it be weal or woe.

Strong in faith, the monks who second
Their Franciscan leader's views
Have the holy-water vessels
Ready to baptize the Jews;

They are waiting for the sprinklers
And their censer soon arrives—
And meanwhile their adversaries
Whet the circumcision knives.

In the hall, at battle-ready
Both the factions stand around;
The impatient crowd is waiting
For the starting bell to sound.

15   Underneath a golden awning
Where the courtiers swarm and swirl,
There the king and queen are sitting—
She is like a little girl.

There's a Gallic little snub nose,
Roguish giggles on her face,
And enchanting are her lips where
Smiling rubies glow with grace.

Beautiful and fragile flower—
May God shield her from all pain!—
Hapless girl, to be transplanted
From the gay banks of the Seine

To the stiff and starchy circles
Of Castile's highborn grandees;
Once called Blanche of Bourbon, now it's
Donna Blanca, if you please.

Pedro is the king's name—he is
Called "the Cruel" by his foes;
But today his mood is milder
Than this appellation shows.

20   He behaves with high good humor
Midst the courtiers en bloc;
For the Jews and Moors he also
Has civilities in stock.

These foreskinless knights are special
Favored flunkeys of the king's:

They command his armies, and they
Run finance and suchlike things.

Now a sudden drum roll rumbles
And the trumpets loud proclaim
That the oral contest's starting,
With two athletes in the game.

The Franciscan head, commencing
In a pious rage, combines
Both a tone of vulgar bluster
With a trick of noisome whines.

In the name of Father, Son and
Holy Ghost, he exorcises
Both the rabbi and all Jacob's
Cursèd seed in all its guises;

25   For in such debates one finds that
Little devils often hide
In the Jews, and give them sharpened
Wits and arguments beside.

Having thus expelled the devils
By the might of exorcism,
Now the monk takes up dogmatics
And fires off the catechism.

He explains that in the Godhead
There are three personae—three—
Who, however, when convenient
Turn into a Unity.

It's a mystery that only
Can be grasped if you dispense
With the reason's mental shackles
And the prison house of sense.

He explains that God was born at
Bethlehem, conceived in fact
By the Virgin, who kept always
Her virginity intact;

30   How the Lord lay in the manger,
Calf and heifer at his side
Standing by devout and pious—
Two dumb cattle, oxen-eyed.

He explained the Lord fled Herod's
Myrmidons, to the domain
Of old Egyptland, and later
Suffered death's most cruel pain

Under Pilate who agreed to
Sign the sentence, so to please
All the Jews who drove him to it,
The hardhearted Pharisees.

He explained how God had risen
From his grave of rayless night
On the third day of his death, and
Up to Heaven took his flight;

And how, comes the time, however,
He'll return with awesome tread
To Jehoshaphat for judgment
Of the living and the dead.

35   "Tremble, Jews," the friar thundered,
"At the God you heaped with woes,
Whom your crown of thorns once martyred,
Whom you drove to death with blows.

"Jews, you ever-vengeful people,
As His killers we esteem you—

And you always kill the Saviour
When He comes here to redeem you.

"Jews, you are a living carcass
In which demons live and revel,
And your bodies are a barracks
For the legions of the Devil.

"Thomas of Aquino says so,
He who's called the Mighty Ox
Of the scholars—he is truly
Glory of the orthodox.

"Jews, you're wolves, you are hyenas,
Jackals grubbing into graves,
Thirsting for the blood of corpses
That your greedy spirit craves.

40   "Jews, O Jews, you're hogs, you're monkeys,
Vile baboons, and dirty rats,
Hornèd-nose rhinoceroses,
Crocodiles, and vampire bats.

"You are hoot owls, hawks, and hoopoes,
Vultures tearing carrion turds,
Basilisks and cockatrices,
Hideous harpies, gallows birds.

"You are crawly worms and vipers,
Rattlesnakes, and slimy eels,
Toads and adders—Christ will grind your
Cursèd heads beneath His heels.

"Or, you cursèd wretches, would you
Save your souls as Jesus showed?
Flee the synagogue of evil,
Fly to Jesus' blest abode,

"To the light of Love's cathedral
Where the fount of grace flows fair

Into Heaven-hallowed basins—
Stick your sinful heads in there—

45   "Then you'll wash out the old Adam
And his vices black as coal,
All your ancient spite and rancor—
Wash its mould from heart and soul!

"Don't you hear the Saviour calling
Your new name to glory in?
Get deloused on Jesus' bosom
From the vermin known as Sin!

"Oh, our God is love incarnate,
Gentle as a lamb is He;
To atone for our offenses
Did He die on Calvary.

"Oh, our God is love incarnate,
Jesus Christ his gloried name;
To reflect His humble meekness
And His patience is our aim.

"Hence we too are calm and gentle,
Never wrangling, ever mild,
Like the Lamb of Peace, our model,
Sunny-tempered as a child.

50   "We will one day walk in Heaven
With the holy angel bands,
In a bliss that's beatific
With white lilies in our hands.

"No more monkish cowls for us then,
But the finest-looking clothes
Of brocade and silk and muslin,
Golden tassels, ribboned bows.

"No more tonsures! Golden locks will
Wreathe our heads, and lovely maids

Will be busily adorning
Our coiffures with handsome braids.

"Up there, all the wine cups will be
Of much bigger, better shapes
Than the goblets here below that
Hold the juice of earthly grapes.

"But contrariwise a lady's
Mouth will be much more petite
Up in Heaven than the earthly
Ones we're now more apt to meet.

55   "Drinking, kissing, laughing, we will
Have Eternity to spend
Singing glory-hallelujahs
And hosannas without end."

Thus the Christian closed. The friars,
Sure that no remaining doubt
Could becloud a single bosom,
Dragged baptismal basins out.

But the Jews grinned scornful grins and
Still remained as water-shy.
Rabbi Judah of Navarre now
Rose to render his reply:

"To manure the seed you're sowing
In my spirit's barren ground,
You load up your dung with insults
And spread barrelsful around.

"Everyone to his own method:
Each man does what he knows how;
I won't chide you for it—thank you,
I'm resigned to it by now.

60   "But this Trinitarian doctrine
Will not do at all, you see,

For a people who since childhood
Have dealt with the Rule of Three.

"That your Godhead has three persons,
And three only, is a claim
That is moderate: the ancients
Knew six thousand gods by name.

"I don't know this 'Christ' you talk of—
I suppose, some god or other;
Nor have I yet had the honor
To have known his Virgin Mother.

"That, twelve hundred years ago
In Jerusalem, he clearly
Had unpleasant tribulations—
I regret this most sincerely.

"That it was the Jews who killed him
Is a hard thing to say now
Since the *corpus delicti* vanished
Three days afterward somehow.

65   "Claims that he is some relation
To our own God can't be so,
For the latter has no children,
Far as any of us know.

"It was not our Lord who perished
Like your wretched Lamb of God
For humanity—he is no
Foolish-philanthropic clod.

"No, our God's not love incarnate,
Never bills and coos—no wonder,
For he is a God of vengeance
And he is a God of thunder.

"His stern lightning smites each sinner
And his wrath is grim and gruff;

And a father's guilt is paid for
By the children oft enough.

"Our God is a living God:
Up in Heaven's spaces, he
Lives in glory and will live on
All through far Eternity.

70   "Our God is a healthy God:
Not mere legend to affright us,
Thin as a communion wafer,
Pale as shadows on Cocytus.

"Strong is he. His hands keep planets,
Suns and stars upon their path;
Thrones are toppled, nations perish
When he knits his brow in wrath.

"And he is a mighty God.
David sang at his behest:
Never can his might be measured,
Earth's a footstool for his rest.

"Our God loves the sound of music,
Festal song and singing strings;
But it jars, like piglets grunting,
When an odious church bell rings.

"There's the fish, Leviathan,
Dwelling deep beneath the sea;
For an hour each day the Lord
Frolics with him sportively—

75   "Every day except the ninth
Day of Ab, the day of woe,
When his temple lay in ashes;
On that day he feels too low.

"This Leviathan's a hundred
Miles in length of giant whale,

Fins as big as Og of Bashan,
Huge as cedars is his tail.

"But his flesh is tasty, more so
Than a turtle's fresh from shore;
On the day of resurrection
God will spread a table for

"All the pious, wise, and upright
Chosen souls from everywhere—
And the Lord God's favorite fish will
Furnish out the bill of fare,

"Partly with white garlic gravy,
Partly in a well-browned roux
Made with spicy wine and raisins—
Something like a seafood stew.

80 "Sizzling in the garlic gravy,
Bits of radish fizz and hiss—
I would wager, friar, you would
Relish fish prepared like this!

"Or the brown one—it's delicious
Raisin sauce right off the fire;
It would make a little Heaven
In your belly, dearest friar.

"God's cuisine is haute cuisine;
Take my counsel with élan:
Give them that old scrap of foreskin
And enjoy Leviathan."

Thus the rabbi—tempting, baiting,
Inly grinning at his ploy;
And the Jews were all ready
Waving knives with grunts of joy,

Set to scalp the forfeit foreskins
Due to victors as their right—

Truly *spolia opima*
In this most peculiar fight.

85   But the monks clung to their natal
Faith and foreskins, in this matter;
They would not be separated
From the former or the latter.

When the Jew was through, the friar
Once more started. He exploded
Into insults: every statement
Was a chamberpot—and loaded.

Then the rabbi answered calmly,
Damping down his zealot's fire;
Though his heart was boiling over,
Yet he checked his rising ire.

He called on the Mishna's teachings,
Commentaries, notes, and tracts,
Citing from the Tousfes Yontov
Many cogent quotes and facts.

But upon his ruffled hearing,
Ah, what blasphemies now fall!
Cries the monk: "The Tousfes Yontov
Doesn't mean a thing at all."

90   "That's the living end, oh God!"
Screams the rabbi, piqued and pale;
Suddenly his patience leaves him
And his mind goes off the rail.

"If you scrap the Tausfes Yontov,
What is left? Oh my, oh me!
Scourge, O Lord, this evildoer,
Punish this iniquity!

"For the Tausfes Yontov, God,
Is thyself! Avenge this shame,
Smite this Tousfes Yontov scorner,
Clear the honor of thy name.

"Let the pit that swallowed Korah
And his evil company
Yawn for him who hatches complots
To defy thy law and thee.

"Thunder out thy loudest thunder!
Punish him, O Lord God, for a
Crime like this, as pitch and brimstone
Rained on Sodom and Gomorrah!

95 "Smite the Capuchins, O Lord God,
As thine arm smote Pharaoh's packs
When they pressed pursuit on us who
Fled with heavy-laden sacks.

"Knights, a hundred thousand, followed
This proud king of the *Mizrayim*,
Mailed in iron, sabers gleaming
In their terrible *yadayim*.

"Lord, thy *yad* was stretched above them,
And it smote them on the head. See—
All that host were drowned like kittens
With their Pharaoh in the Red Sea.

"Smite the Capuchins, O Lord God,
Show these scoundrels living proof
That the lightnings of thine anger
Haven't fizzled to a *poof.*

"Then I'll sing the praise and glory
Of thy might, thy worshiper;

And I'll dance, as Miriam did once,
And I'll beat the drum, like her."

100   Here the monk broke in with anger
As his fury sizzled through:
"May the Lord destroy you, damn you,
May He heap His curse on you!

"I defy your insect devils,
All your dirty gods of death,
Lucifer, Beelzebub,
Belial, and Ashtoreth.

"I defy your hellish spirits,
All their tricks are cheap and shoddy,
For within me is Christ Jesus,
I've partaken of His body.

"Christ's my favorite dish, much better
Than Leviathan-in-a-pot,
Even with white garlic gravy
Made by Satan, like as not.

"Oh! instead of wrangling, I would
Rather roast you on a fire,
Stew you and your comrades with you
On the hottest funeral pyre."

105   Thus with insults and grave charges
Raged the joust for Faith and God,
But in vain the champions scolded,
Screamed and raged and oh'd and ah'd.

Now the fight's gone on twelve hours
With no end in sight, not yet;
And the audience grows weary,
And the women swim in sweat.

And the court, too, grows impatient,
Servants yawning hollow-eyed;
Then the king turns with a question
To the fair queen at his side:

"Tell me, what is your opinion?
Which of them is in the right?
Do you think it is the rabbi
Or the monk that's won the fight?"

Donna Blanca gazes at him,
Fingers twined and hands pressed fast
To her forehead, as if musing,
And then this she says at last:

110   "I don't know which one is right—
But I'll tell you what I think
Of the rabbi and the friar:
Both of them alike, they stink."

Notes and Variants

NOTES TO THE RABBI OF BACHERACH

The RABBI OF BACHERACH was published in 1840 in the fourth volume of the series SALON. Heine had started work on this novella in 1824; whether he ever completed it is not certain. Heine himself said that the manuscript was burned during a fire in his mother's house in Hamburg. He referred to the published RABBI OF BACHERACH as a fragment.

The text of this volume is based on the translation from the German by Charles Godfrey Leland (New York: E. P. Dutton & Co. and London: William Heinemann, 1906). While Leland's translation captures the poetic language of Heine, certain passages, especially those describing Jewish customs, were imprecise. For our edition, Elizabeth Petuchowski has reworded the Leland translation wherever necessary.

The reproductions of the lithographs by the renowned Berlin artist Max Liebermann are from the Berlin 1923 Propyläen edition. Liebermann signed all 400 copies of this limited edition, which is considered to be an outstanding example of German book art. The Heinrich Heine Institute in Düsseldorf has graciously supplied reproductions of the Liebermann drawings for this edition and as well as photographic reproductions showing Heine and his time.

Footnotes by Leland are quoted with his name in brackets.

Page

21   *Bacharach* = Bacherach: stems from Ara Bacchi, the altar of Bacchus, on account of the wine made there. "A jolly place it was in days of yore; But something ails it now- the spot is cursed." [Leland]
Leland updated the spelling of Bacherach to conform to the now usual practice of "Bacharach." "Bach-erach" was already an archaic form in Heine's own day and the poet chose this spelling deliberately. Heine's preference is honored in this edition.

25   *Agade:* Heine meant the *HAGGADAH* (from Hebrew *higgid* = to tell) for Passover, the volume containing the liturgy for the domestic Passover evening ser-vice(s), with psalms and songs, prayers and narrative passages pertaining to the exodus from Egypt. The form *Aggadah* (from the Aramaic) is now reserved for the non-legal portions of scripture exegesis in the broadest sense. The final -*e* (instead of -*ah*) suggests that Heine was familiar with the German-Ashkenazi pronunciation.

28   *Mitzri:* Egyptian.

32   *Schadai.* Almighty God.

34   *canoe:* The Rhine boats were almost invariably ca-noe-like in form. *Whereon joy grows.* An allusion to the vineyards of the Rhine. [Leland]

37   *leafy tabernacles:* reference to the Succoth, built by Jews to celebrate the harvest festival, the Feast of Tabernacles.
Now I must go to Spain Medieval Spain was the center of Jewish culture and learning, producing fa-mous physicians, philosophers and poets, among them Jehuda ha-Levi and Ibn Ezra (see "Hebrew Melodies"). Some prominent Spanish Jews achieved positions as diplomats, interpreters and overseas

merchants at the courts of the Spanish kings. Ever since then, Jews of Spanish and Portuguese provenance have been held in high regard by other Jews. Heine had acquainted himself with Spanish-Jewish biographies.

39 *Great flowers with marvelous broad spreading foliage:* The whole spirit of Gothic decoration, of grotesque figures and faces, twined about with vines and crochets, or expanded leaves exaggerated into strange yet beautiful forms, is given in this passage. [Leland]

41 *Ten thousand to the right:* Allusion to the Jewish Prayer Before Retiring at Night, based on Song of Songs.

43 Starting in 1498, the Jews of Frankfurt were forced to pay the "Rattenpfennig," a payment to fight rats.

44 The Venetians pushed their wares into Paris, Rome and Germany with all the enterprise of modern commercial travelers. [Leland]

45 *Römer:* the most famous building in Frankfurt.

49 *Lumpenbrunnen:* Rag Fountain; *Mehlwaage:* Flour Scale; *Wollgraben:* Wool Ditch (street where the weavers worked).

50 *Flagellants:* religious fanatics in the Middle Ages who practiced self-castigation as a religious rite.

50 *Schnozzle Stern:* German: Nasenstern. The popular Jewish name Stern translates into English as Star. The combination of the name Stern with the German word for "nose" yields the nickname Nasenstern.

51 *Rindskopf:* English: Oxhead (nickname). Cruel nicknames were common in the Middle Ages.

51 *Prayer of Eighteen Benedictions:* The Prayer *par excellence* in Jewish liturgy. It has eighteen benedic-

tions on weekdays, fewer on Sabbath and Holidays, but is even then called *Prayer of Eighteen Benedictions.*

55   *A kid, a kid . . . :* Concluding song of the *Haggadah.* Heine eliminated its culminating stanza: "There came the Holy One and killed the angel of death . . ."

56   *Edom:* A state neighboring Judea in biblical times, and a rival nation. Hence, the name Edom has been used to symbolize all enemies of the Jews.
      Ellen Schnapper is Heine's Schnapper Elle. It is possible in German colloquial language to use the family name first.
      which looketh forth to Damascus: Heine parodies images of the biblical Song of Songs.

59   *great fire:* the great fire in the Jewish quarter of Frankfurt occurred in 1711.

66   *Midian and Moab:* the animosity of the Midianites and Moabites, two neighboring tribes in biblical times, became proverbial among the Jews.

75   *Astarte:* Phoenician goddess of fertility.

NOTES TO SHYLOCK

The essay *Shylock* was originally published under the title *Jessica* as part of the collection *Shakespeare's Maidens and Women*

. . . *Franz Horn:* Literary historian and Shakespearean critic (1781–1837) 'Les blancs l'ont tué' The white men have killed Him; let us kill the white men!' Heine is referring to the 1791 massacre of San Domingo, when the Chris-

tian black slaves revolted against their white oppressors
and eventually created the first black state of Haiti in 1804.

Notes by Hal Draper
on
HEBREW MELODIES

H. took this title from Byron's *Hebrew Melodies,*
published in 1815, though the similarity is otherwise
not great.

97a [Motto] *O lass nicht ohne Lebensgenuss . . .*—Orig-
inal ms title: 'Album Leaf.'

97b Prinzessin Sabbat. *In Arabiens Märchen-
buche . . .*—The personification of the Sabbath as a
beautiful woman is taken by Heine from the Hebrew
poem which he praises in **St. 15–17,** and which he
ascribes to Judah Halevy; but it was actually written
much later by a 16th-century Cabbalist named Sol-
omon Halevy Alkabez. In the Hebrew poem, which
became part of the Jewish liturgy, it is a question not
of a princess but of a bride. A German translation of
this song, beginning 'Komme, Freund, der Braut ent-
gegen, lass uns den Sabbat begrüssen,' was found
among Heine's papers and was long considered to be
his own. But it was probably translated for him by a
friend. Although **St. 16** purports to quote the begin-
ning of the poem, this poem actually commences as
follows: "Come, friend, to meet the bride, let us
welcome the Sabbath! / *Schamor* [observance] and
Sachor [remembrance] did the one God make known
to us in a single Word [commandment], / God is one
and His name is one; let us praise and glorify Him!"
(This follows the German version used by Heine, but
with an eye on a literal translation from the Hebrew

made for me by an erudite friend.)—Throughout this and the next poem, I have retained the form of the name which Heine gives Halevy. "Jehuda ben Halevy," since it is indispensable to the meter. However, it is, strictly speaking, incorrect; his patronymic was ben Samuel, and his full name was Judah (or Jehuda) ben Samuel Halevy (or Halevi, ha-Levi, that is, the Levite). In **St. 17,** Heine uses the Spanish "Don" for Judah Halevy in order to mark his Spanish birth, but at the same time he equates his love poems with those of the German minnesingers. For Halevy's life, see the notes on the next poem.—It should be borne in mind that, throughout this poem, Heine, through the prince/princess allegory, is describing the actual Sabbath observance. In St. 8, the words represent what the worshiper says ritually on entering the synagogue; in **St. 36,** the box of spices is handed around as part of the closing ritual; and so on.

St. 1. Arabia's book of fables: the Thousand and One Nights. **St. 6.** The Jewish sabbath begins and ends at sundown. **St. 15—16.** The Hebrew line is given here in its Ashkenazic form, which is also indicated by Heine's own transliteration. **St. 26, L. 1–2.** Schiller's 'Ode to Joy' is parodied here, the words having been made doubly famous in 1823 by Beethoven's Ninth Symphony.

102 Jehuda ben Halevy. *Lechzend klebe mir die Zunge . . .*—Judah Halevy was a Jewish rabbi, poet, and philosopher. Born about 1085 in Toledo, Spain, he was one of the greatest Hebrew poets of the Middle Ages. He died, about 1140, on a pilgrimage to Jerusalem, perhaps near it; the story that he was slain by an Arab near Jerusalem was a much-repeated legend, which H. further embroiders with fictional details.— H.'s main source was Michael Sachs' book *Die re-*

ligiöse Poesie der Juden in Spanien (1845), which also provided German translations of selections from Halevy and two other poets stressed by Sachs (and by H. in this poem): Solomon ben Judah Ibn Gabirol, born at Malaga, and Moses Ibn Ezra of Granada. (Browning's Rabbi ben Ezra was a relative of the second.)—H.'s notation "Fragment" at the end of the poem indicates that he regarded it as unfinished.—In the poem, I have retained the form of the name used by Heine, even though it is incorrect, as explained in the note to the preceding poem.

102 [The same] Part i. *Lechzend klebe mir die Zunge* . . . St. 1. The quotation is based on Psalms; but I have followed Heine's version here. St. 7. This indication of Halevy's year of birth is an error taken over from Sachs. St. 13. Shalsheleth: a combination of tones in the reading of the Torah. St. 14. Targum: a translation (ca. 100–130) of the Pentateuch into Aramaic, reputedly by Onkelos (perhaps a fictitious name). St. 15. Garlic-sausage Hebrew: H. writes "gillyflower-Hebrew," making an association with the "Swabian" German of the preceding line; compare 'Atta Troll' where "gillyflowers" and "sausage soup" are representative of Swabian homeyness. In other words, H. is saying that Aramaic is to Hebrew as Swabian is to German. St. 17. Halacha: the exposition of legislative injunctions in the Talmud, often in hairsplitting fashion. St. 18. H. wrote "athletes of Babylonia and Pumbedita," but Pumbedita was *in* Babylonia (it was one of two Babylonian cities with important Jewish academies). St. 19. Kuzari: Halevy's most important work on Judaism. St. 21. Haggada: the didactic part of the Talmud using much poetic, legendary and allegorical material. Halacha: See St. 17 above.

108 [The same] Part ii. *Bei den Wassern Babels sassen . . .*   St. 1. as in Part i, the first stanza is again a quotation from *Psalms*, 137, lines 1–2; again I follow H.'s version here. St. 7. Without using quote marks, H. is again quoting from the 137th Psalm, which ends, "Happy shall he be, that taketh and dasheth thy little ones against the stones." The reference is to the "children of Edom" and Babylonians who advocated the razing of Jerusalem. St. 8. Western-Eastern: cf Goethe's *Western-Eastern Divan*, poems of 1819, implying a fusion of Western and Oriental elements. Here H. suggests the tensions implicit in a dual heritage. St. 12. Sirvente: type of Provençal song much used by troubadours for moral satire. Ghazel: a type of erotic Arabic lyric. St. 14. These are all parts of France (especially old Aquitaine) associated with troubadour activity. St. 15. In ms, "remembrance" is replaced by "Romanticism." St. 21. Laura: Petrarch's lady love, whom the poet saw in a church one day (but not on Good Friday). St. 23. The reference is to the alleged *cours d'amour* described in troubadour poetry. St. 24. Jerusalem had been destroyed twice—in 586 B.C. by Nebuchadnezzar, and in 70 A.D. by Titus. St. 28. Pilgrim: the legendary Wandering Jew (Ahasuerus). St. 36. Ninth of Ab: the date, in the Jewish calendar, of the destruction of Jerusalem by Titus in 70 A.D. St. 39–45. For Geoffrey Rudel of Blaye (here given the title of Vidame, one of the lesser nobles) and Melisande. St. 43. Cette (now Sète): a Mediterranean port on the Languedoc coast of France. St. 47. In H.'s first ms. version, this is replaced by three stanzas in which he invents a new version of Halevy's death:

> And Jehuda ben Halevy,
> Also driven, went abroad on

A felucca run by Spaniards
Which transported him to Cairo.

With a caravan he traveled
From far Egypt to Arabia;
After wandering the desert
Came he to Jerusalem.

He sat on the temple's ruins
Singing his illustrious *Kinah*,
His great song of lamentation,
"Zion," when the death-spear slew him.

114 [The same] Part iii. *Nach der Schlacht bei Arabella . . .* **St. 1.** Arbela (in Assyria): the battle in which Alexander overthrew Darius III in 331 B.C., actually fought at Gaugamela, sixty miles away. H. gives the name as "Arabella" perhaps for metrical reasons. **St. 8.** Rump-thumper *[Arschpauker]:* that is, schoolmaster. **St. 9.** Smerdis, who was the second son of Cyrus the Great of Persia, was assassinated by his brother Cambyses II, who kept his death secret. Cambyses was himself deposed and replaced by one Guamata posing as Smerdis; the false Smerdis reigned for seven months. Atossa, Cyrus' daughter, was first married to Cambyses, then to the false Smerdis. **St. 10–13.** Thaïs: a 4th century B.C. Athenian courtesan, of doubtful historicity, said to have been Alexander's mistress and to have inspired him to burn Persepolis. (This is not the later Thaïs celebrated by Anatole France.) **St. 13.** Babylonian ailment: venereal disease. **St. 13–22.** Walzel points out that this history of the pearls resembles the story of Roland's nuptial bed in Ariosto. **St. 16–17.** Omayyads, Abderam: for the Moors in Spain. In 'Almansor,' the last of the Omayyads was more properly called Abd al-Rahman. **St. 21.** Mendizábal:

head of the Spanish government who in 1836 found a drastic solution for the crushing national debt through the confiscation and sale of church and monastic property; he was of Jewish descent. **St. 22.** Madame Solomon the baroness: wife of Solomon Rothschild, head of the Vienna branch of the family. **St. 24.** Plutarch relates that Alexander kept Homer's work under his pillow at night. **St. 46.** H. wrote: "by Titus Vespasianus." Vespasian's son Titus, who conquered Jerusalem, became emperor after this exploit. **St. 55.** The "ancient legend" is of H.'s invention. **St. 59—61.** For this Sabbath song, which was not written by Halevy, see the notes to 'Princess Sabbath' above.

122 [The same]. Part iv. *Meine Frau ist nicht zufrieden . . .* **St. 5.** Marquis: a shop in Paris. **St. 7.** H. here opens quote marks which are closed only at the end of the poem; I have omitted this set of marks. **St. 14.** The reader should remember that H. did not know much Hebrew. **St. 17—20.** Rabbi Judah ben Solomon Alcharisi wrote his book entitled *Tachkemoni* in the style of the *Makamat* of Hariri, an Arab poet; the *makamas* by Hariri were written mainly in rhymed prose. **St. 21—30.** That Ibn Ezra was a cousin of Halevy's was H.'s invention. The story about Ibn Ezra was embroidered by H. from some details in Sachs' book. **St. 32 et sqq.** Schlemihl: a Yiddish term, made famous by Chamisso's tale *The Wonderful Story of Peter Schlemihl*, who sold his shadow to the devil; written in 1813, partly to amuse the children of his friend, Hitzig. Chamisso explained in a letter: "*Schlemihl*, or better *Schlemiel*, is a Hebrew name and means the same as Gottlieb, Théophile, 'beloved of God.' In the common speech of the Jews it designates clumsy and ill-starred people, who

cannot do the slightest thing successfully. A Schlemihl breaks a finger in a vest-pocket; he falls on his back and breaks his nose; he always comes at the wrong time. Schlemihl, whose name became a byword, is a person of whom the Talmud tells the following story: 'He was seeing a rabbi's wife, but let himself get caught at it, and was killed.' . . .'' **St. 34.** H's thrust here is at the fact that Jews did not have equal civic rights. **St. 37.** Julius Eduard Hitzig: friend and biographer of Chamisso, who dedicated the Peter Schlemihl story to him. As H. indicates, Hitzig was of Jewish birth, converted early, and became a *Kriminalrat* in Berlin. **St. 40.** H. is punning on *Heilige* (saint) and *heilige* (holy). **St. 61.** Fama: in Roman myth, usually Rumor; H. probably means Fame. **St. 62 to end.** The story of Gabirol's death is from Sachs.

131 Disputation. *In der Aula zu Toledo* . . . (Wr) August 1851, just before sending *Romancero* to the publisher.—Original title: 'Controversy.'—The public disputation, an institution known in France and Spain, was a formal debate between a Jewish and a Christian theological champion (the former usually performing under duress), designed to foster conversion of Jews. H. read about it in Basnage's *Histoire de la Religion des Juifs* (1707). But the disputation described here is not historical. It is set in the time of Pedro I of Castile and León and his queen Blanche of Bourbon (Blanca in Spain). Pedro married Blanche, under pressure, in 1354 but soon deserted her, and it is not likely they held court together (as depicted by H.). Besides, Pedro was friendly to the Jews, whom he used as tax-gatherers.—H. wrote this poem with great speed, and it has numerous anachronisms, for example, the ref-

erence to the "Tausfes Yontov" (see note on St. 88
below).   **St. 3.** Capuchins: a branch of the Fran-
ciscan monks. **St. 4.** Arbakanfos (or Arba Kanfos,
"four corners"): a fringed cloth ritually worn by male
orthodox Jews. The scapular, worn somewhat sim-
ilarly, was a badge of the monastic order. **St. 21.** In
ms, H. had enlarged on the Jewish "flunkeys" of the
king by replacing this stanza with two:

These foreskinless nobles were the
Sort the king was partial to,
And they were of service to him,
Faithful subjects tried and true;

Filled his treasure bags, and fought
In his army, staunch and brave,
Till Don Henry the Infante
Sent him to an early grave.

St. 38. Thomas of Aquino (or Thomas von Aquin):
the common German form of Thomas Aquinas; Aqui-
no was the family name. He was more usually called
the Dumb Ox, not Mighty Ox. **St. 45–46.** In ms,
these two stanzas were replaced by one:

Then wash out of heart and soul
All the ancient mould of spite
And the vermin of your sins, so
Heaven's gates will open bright—

St. 60–61. In ms, these stanzas were replaced by:

This is your Trinity mystery
We'll discuss some other season
When the moon's in its first quarter
And I'm less disposed to reason

Than in daytime's sober brightness
Where the sunlight's plain to see,

When the Rule of Three holds sway
In its dry reality.

St. 66. The fourth line uses an untranslatable portmanteau word *Philantröpchen*, which telescopes *Philanthrop* into the diminutive of *Tropf* (ninny). **St. 70.** Cocytus: a river in Hades. **St. 72.** David sang: an error; the reference is mainly to *Isaiah*. **St. 74.** The feast on Leviathan's flesh is based on rabbinical tradition. **St. 75.** Ninth of Ab: anniversary of the destruction of Jerusalem by Titus in 70 A.D. **St. 83–84.** In the ms version:

Thus the rabbi—tempting, baiting,
Like the snake in Paradise—
As if after a rich dinner
Licked his fingers once or twice.

Shivering with joy, the Jews were
Thinking that they soon would win,
And they grabbed the knives, the better
Circumcision to begin.

St. 84. Spolia opima: rich booty. **St. 88.** Mishna: first of the two parts of the Talmud, containing the oral law (body of traditional teachings). Tausfes Yontov (in Heine, *Tausves-Jontow*): corruption of the name of a commentary on the Mishna by Yom Tobh Lipmann Heller which was published in 1614, the book being titled *Tosaphoth Yom Tobh;* it is not as important as H.'s rabbi claims. As mentioned, a discussion in the 14th century could not have referred to this 17th century work. **St. 93.** Korah: See *Numbers*, 16. **St. 96–97.** *Mizrayim:* Egyptians (in Hebrew). *Yadayim:* hands (in Hebrew); *yad* (**in St. 97**) is singular.